HEROES OF HISTORY

LAURA INGALLS WILDER

A Storybook Life

HEROES OF HISTORY

LAURA INGALLS WILDER

A Storybook Life

JANET & GEOFF BENGE

Emerald
Books

P.O. BOX 635, LYNNWOOD, WA 98046

Emerald Books are distributed through YWAM Publishing. For a full list of titles, including other great biographies, visit our website at www.ywampublishing.com or call 1-800-922-2143.

Library of Congress Cataloging-in-Publication Data

Benge, Janet, 1958–
     Laura Ingalls Wilder : a storybook life / Janet and Geoff Benge.
        p. cm. — (Heroes of history)
     Includes bibliographical references.
     ISBN 1-932096-32-9
     1. Wilder, Laura Ingalls, 1867–1957. 2. Authors, American—
20th century—Biography. 3. Women pioneers—United States—
Biography. 4. Frontier and pioneer life—United States.
5. Children's stories—Authorship. I. Benge, Geoff, 1954–
II. Title. III. Series: Benge, Janet, 1958– Heroes of history.
     PS3545.I342Z569 2005
     813'.52—dc22
     [B]
                                                        2005020395

Published by Emerald Books
P.O. Box 635
Lynnwood, Washington 98046

ISBN 1-932096-32-9

Printed in the United States of America.

HEROES OF HISTORY
Biographies

Abraham Lincoln
Benjamin Franklin
Christopher Columbus
Clara Barton
Daniel Boone
Douglas MacArthur
George Washington
George Washington Carver
Harriet Tubman
John Adams
Laura Ingalls Wilder
Meriwether Lewis
Theodore Roosevelt
William Penn

More Heroes of History coming soon!
Unit study curriculum guides are available
for select biographies.

Available at your local bookstore or
through Emerald Books
1 (800) 922-2143

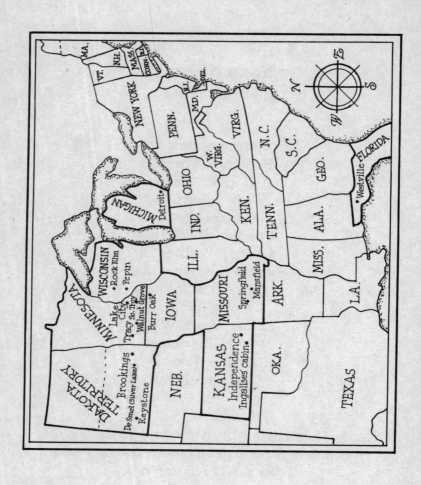

Contents

1. The Family Storyteller 9
2. On the Prairie 13
3. Moving On 25
4. A New Life in the Wisconsin Woods 39
5. A Christmas Surprise 51
6. A Sugar Snow 63
7. On the Banks of Plum Creek 77
8. The Strange Cloud 89
9. Burr Oak 103
10. Working on the Railroad 115
11. The Long Winter 131
12. A Quiet, Steady Man 145
13. Joy and Sorrow 157
14. A Real Home 171
15. Old Things Passing Away 181
    Bibliography 195

Chapter 1

The Family Storyteller

The scene was hard for Laura Ingalls Wilder to take in as she stood to speak at the 1937 Detroit Children's Book Fair. The place was packed with people who had come to hear her speak and have her autograph their copies of her books. Laura felt anxious. She had never spoken to such a large crowd. After all, what did she have to say—she was just a farmer's wife from Missouri. She had been content in that role all her life, and she still thought of herself that way. Then one day she had put pen to paper and had begun to write down some of the stories from her youth. She had no idea when she started whether people would even want to read her stories, but they did, and now she was a famous author. And that was why the crowd was pressing in to the book fair—to catch a glimpse of her and listen to what she had to say.

It was all a little odd, really, and if the truth be told, Laura would much rather have been back home on the farm, feeding the cows, than standing in front of this crowd. On the farm she felt happy and secure, not anxious and exposed as she did right now. But her publisher had wanted her to attend the Children's Book Fair, so here she was, for better or for worse, ready to speak to the crowd.

Laura had to admit to herself that it was flattering that so many people had shown up to hear her. But the two people she would have wanted most to be there were not. They were both long since dead, buried side by side in a cemetery in South Dakota, but it was because of them that she was here today in Detroit. Ma and Pa Ingalls were responsible for her being who she was. The years Laura had spent growing up with them on the prairie had shaped Laura's character and molded her. It was they who had taught her the importance of getting an education, of picking yourself up and going on after you have been knocked down by life's misfortunes, of being cheerful and courageous, and of finding the little, everyday pleasures in life. And these were all the lessons Laura had tried to communicate through her stories of life growing up on the prairie.

As the moderator introduced her, how Laura wished that Ma and Pa could see her now. They had died before she had ever put pen to paper. Ma had always made sure that Laura and her sisters attended school when they could and that at least one or two books were always in the house to read. And how proud Pa would be. Pa had always been the family storyteller, and Laura could still hear his voice and booming laugh. But while Pa had held her spellbound as a child with his stories, fate had made her, Laura, the teller of the Ingalls family saga of life on the prairie. And what a saga it had been.

Chapter 2

On the Prairie

Laura Ingalls sat on the doorstep, looking out across the endless prairie. Even though the morning sun was still low in the eastern sky, she could feel its warmth on her face. At any moment she expected her mother to call her to put on her sunbonnet so that her skin did not burn in the baking sun. But somehow her mother seemed strangely preoccupied this morning.

"Now you just sit there on that rocking chair and don't mind a thing," Laura heard Pa say to her mother. She peered inside the log cabin. The milk from the cow was sitting unchurned in the bucket beside the table, and the bowls from breakfast had not yet been put back up high on the shelf. That was odd. Laura's mother usually took care of such things straightaway. Something was definitely different about this August morning.

"How about we go explore an Indian camp, girls?" Pa asked.

"Could we, Pa? All four of us?" Laura heard her older sister Mary ask, and then she caught a look of amusement pass between her parents.

"Just the three of us today, girls. Mrs. Scott is coming over to visit with your mother, and I thought that you'd like an adventure," Pa said.

"Yes, yes, I would!" three-and-a-half-year-old Laura exclaimed. Even at this young age she wanted to see what lay beyond the circle of prairie that enveloped the family and their log cabin. "Can Jack come too? He loves chasing jackrabbits and squirrels."

"How about it, Caroline?" Pa asked Laura's mother. "If I take Jack, I'll leave you with the rifle, and Mrs. Scott should be carrying one too."

"That's fine. You all run along and have a good time," Laura's mother said as she placed straw sunbonnets on the girls' heads and tied them firmly under their chins.

Soon the two girls waved good-bye to their mother and walked out onto the prairie. Apart from an old Osage Indian trail, there were no roads or tracks on the land. The nearest neighbors, the Scotts, lived more than a mile away, and the town of Independence lay fourteen miles to the northeast. Laura knew that she had been to Independence before, but she was too young to remember anything about the place. She did know, though, that her family had settled on this land a year earlier and that, in that time, her father had built the sturdy log cabin they now lived in, had plowed some of the prairie near the cabin, and had planted wheat and a vegetable patch. Her father had also built a stable for their two horses, Patty and Pet, to keep them safe from the wildcats and wolves that roamed the land at night.

The only thing that rose above the endless prairie grass was a line of trees in the distance, and Laura knew that the trees bordered a creek. "Is that where we're going?" she asked her father as she bobbed along beside him, two of her steps equaling one of his strides.

"Sure is," Pa replied.

"Will we find Indians?" Laura asked.

Even though she lived in Indian territory—a kind of no-man's-land where both the Indians and the pioneers claimed ownership of the land—Laura had seen only Indian men. More than anything, she wanted to see an Indian baby, or a papoose, as her mother said they were called.

"No, Half Pint," her father replied, using Laura's nickname. "It's midsummer, and the Indians have taken their ponies and gone west into the high prairie, hunting for buffalo. They'll be back in the fall with meat and hides, and then they'll settle back in for the winter and head out again to hunt in the spring."

"Why'd they do that?" Mary asked.

"It's just the way they live. The high prairie is too cold for them to live on during the winter but just right for hunting buffalo in the summer. And they don't mind moving around," Pa explained.

"Kind of like you!" Laura remarked.

Her father laughed. "I guess I've done my share of that," he said. "It's in the Ingalls blood."

Just then Jack, the bulldog, barked wildly and sprinted off to their left.

"He's having just as much fun as the rest of us. Do you want to be the lookout?" Pa asked.

Laura felt her father's strong arms reach down and swing her up onto his shoulders. This was her favorite place to be, looking down on everything.

"I see him, Pa!" Laura exclaimed. "He's after a squirrel. Oh, and I see the creek too. We're nearly there."

And so they were. Soon Laura was being lifted from her father's shoulders and placed on the track that led down to the creek. Tall bushes lined the track, and Laura was glad to have Jack back at her side.

"You think any of the Indians stayed behind?" Laura whispered to her father.

"No, they all go together," Pa said as they reached an open area beside the creek.

Laura looked around. Directly in front of her was a fire pit with bones scattered around it.

"Look carefully," her father instructed. "We can learn many things from this. What kind of bones do you think these are?"

Mary and Laura studied them.

"They belong to jackrabbits," their father finally told them. "Look at the long leg bones. And see the marks around the fire."

Laura peered at the sandy ground. Sure enough, she could make out footprints; some were big and some were small.

"Two middle-sized moccasins," Pa said, pointing. "They would be Indian women tending the fire. See, one of them must have bent down beside it, because we can see the marks the fringe of her skirt made."

Laura nodded. She was not sure what the marks were, but she was sure of one thing—her Pa was the smartest man in the world, and if he said something was so, then it was.

"Look over here!" Laura yelled as she spotted something shining in the late morning sun. She ran over and pulled a brilliant blue bead out of the dust. "Look, Mary, it's so beautiful."

Mary came running over. "And here's another one!" she exclaimed to Laura.

Much to the girls' amazement and delight, colored beads were scattered all over the Indian campsite. Some were bloodred, while others were white and brown. Pa joined in the hunt for more beads, and before long, several hours had passed. By the time the Ingalls girls had collected a handful of beads each, the sun was casting long shadows over the creek bed. Pa wrapped the beads separately in his handkerchief, and then it was time for them to start for home. The sun was at their backs as they trudged back across the prairie.

"What do you think Ma's been doing while we've been gone all this time?" Mary asked as they walked.

"We'll have to wait and see. Perhaps she'll have a surprise for us," Pa said with a twinkle in his eye.

"Pa, you know something!" Mary exclaimed, and Laura was sure her sister was right.

As they neared the cabin, Mrs. Scott, her hands on her hips, was standing at the door, waiting for them. She had a big smile on her face.

"Why, Mr. Ingalls, I thought you were never coming back!" she laughed. "Come inside. You too, girls."

It felt strange to Laura to have someone else welcoming her into her own home, but she soon forgot about that when she saw her mother tucked in bed.

Mrs. Ingalls sat up and beckoned Laura and Mary over to her. Laura gasped when she got nearer. Lying beside her mother and wrapped in a blanket was a tiny baby. "Ma!" Laura cried. "Is it ours?"

Pa reached down and lifted the little bundle from the bed.

"It's another girl," Caroline Ingalls said.

Pa's eyes shined. "You can't have too many of them!" Pa laughed as he held the baby out for the girls to see. The baby had red, wrinkly skin, and her hair was as black as coal. "Mary and Laura, meet your new sister," Pa added with a flourish.

Laura could not stop staring at the baby. "What's her name?" she asked.

"I think we'll call her Caroline, after your mother," Pa said. "What do you think, Ma?"

Ma nodded. "Sounds like a fine name."

Later that night the two "big" girls took turns holding the baby. Then Laura watched as her mother entered the birth into the big, leather-bound family Bible. Laura's mother had a much neater writing hand than her father, since she had been a schoolteacher before marrying, while Pa had not been to school much as a boy.

"What are you writing?" Laura wanted to know.

"August 3, 1870. Caroline Celeste Ingalls, born in Montgomery County, Kansas," her mother replied. "Caroline is officially an Ingalls now."

"Read me the rest," Laura begged her mother.

Ma's eyes went to the top of the page, and she began to read. "Caroline Lake Quiner was born to Henry and Charlotte Quiner on December 12, 1839, Brookfield, Wisconsin. That's me, of course, and this is your Pa. Charles Phillip Ingalls was born to Lansford and Laura Ingalls, in Cuba, New York, on January 10, 1836."

"And that's my grandma who I'm named after, right, Ma?" Laura inquired. "The baby is named after you, and I am named after my grandma."

"That's right," her mother agreed, "and here you and Mary are, right under our wedding date." She read on from the names in the Bible. "On February 1, 1860, Charles married Caroline Lake Quiner in Concord, Wisconsin. Mary Amelia Ingalls, first child of Charles and Caroline Ingalls, born January 10, 1865, in Pepin, Wisconsin. Laura Elizabeth Ingalls, second child of Charles and Caroline Ingalls, born February 7, 1867, in Pepin, Wisconsin."

"And now you have a third child!" Laura said as she looked over at the baby.

That night as Laura lay in bed, listening to Pa playing happy tunes on his fiddle, she thought,

"What a wonderful day it has been. First the adventure at the Indian camp with Pa, then finding the shiny beads, and now, best of all, a new baby sister."

Not many days after the birth of Caroline, though, Pa's happy tunes were drowned out by a more ominous noise—thump, thump, thump, thump, thump. It was the sound of drums, lots of them, and they were not far away. Laura was in bed the first time she heard them and called out, "Pa, what's that noise?"

Her father was at her bedside in an instant. "Don't worry, Half Pint. The Indians have returned to their camp, though it sounds like there might be more of them than there were before."

Laura studied her father's face in the candlelight. His voice was calm, but his face looked worried.

"Now go to sleep. Didn't Ma say you could help her milk the cow in the morning like a big girl?" her father asked.

Laura nodded and settled back down in her bed. She tried hard to think about the sparkling beads she had found at the Indian camp several days before and the prospect of learning to milk a cow with her mother in the morning, but somehow her mind kept going back to the Indians drumming their songs across the prairie.

Even though Pa had said not to worry, terrible rumors soon spread as far as the Ingallses' cabin. Laura's mother tried to keep them from the girls, but the girls managed to hear pieces of news. The talk that there might be a war between the Indians and the settlers particularly chilled their bones. But what was even more shocking was that Indian men took to visiting the cabin anytime they wanted. They came day or night, and even though they did not speak any English, Laura could see what they were after—food and furs. Pa built a big cupboard with a lock on it for storing the family's supplies, and whenever he went out hunting, he left Ma with a pistol. And when he was away, Ma spent the nights sitting in the rocking chair, the pistol on her lap, listening for any noises.

Laura could not understand why the Indians had become so menacing. In the past her father had hunted near the Indians' camp and never had any fear that they would harm him.

"They are trying to decide what to do," her father explained. "They cannot stay here and live the way they used to. Plowed fields now block their trails, and settlers are using their hunting grounds. Some people say they will fight to get rid of us all, but I hope they will accept the government's offer and move west into the new Indian territories."

"Do you think they will?" Laura asked.

"It's hard to say. That's what all the noise is about. I bet some want to stay and some don't."

The drums at night grew louder and stronger as more Indians joined the band encamped down by the creek. Now Pa hardly left Ma and the children alone at all, and when he did, one of the neighbors came to stay with them.

Finally news reached the Ingallses' log cabin that the Osage Indians had decided to accept the offer of new land on which to live and were preparing to leave their home on the Kansas prairie for good.

"Caroline, come here. And you, too, Mary and Laura," called Pa, who had just gone out to the stable to hitch up the horses Pet and Patty to the plow for a day's work in the fields.

Laura ran outside ahead of her older sister and her mother. Immediately she turned her head in the direction her father was staring. She could scarcely believe her eyes. As far as she could see into the distance, a line of Indians rode on horseback in single file. Jack the dog growled and barked at the column of Indians, and Pa had to swat him before he would be silent. Ma stood in the doorway of the cabin, holding baby Caroline, or Carrie, as everyone was calling her, while Mary stood beside Laura. They all watched as the first horse approached. On its back rode Osage Chief Soldat du Chene, leading his people west. His dark, weathered face was expressionless, and his brown eyes stared straight ahead. He sat straight-backed on his horse and did not even acknowledge Pa when Pa raised his hat to him. Laura was amazed at how still the chief was able to sit on his horse.

Warrior after warrior followed Chief Soldat du Chene. Each sat still and expressionless on his horse, just as the chief had.

Behind the warriors came the women and children, also riding on horseback. Although the women had blankets draped around them, most of the children were naked. Laura stared as they rode by. Despite living close to the Indian camp down by the creek, this was the first time she had seen Indian children. Like the adults, the children sat expressionless on their horses and stared ahead, except for one baby who was tied in a bundle on her mother's back. The baby's coal-black eyes fixed on Laura and continued to stare at her, turning her head to look back when her mother's horse had ridden by. The sight of the baby staring at her seemed to melt Laura's heart, and Laura wanted to reach out and take the child from her mother's back and hold her tight. But the horse carrying the mother and child plodded on.

The column of Osage Indians took several hours to pass the Ingallses' cabin. And even when they had passed, Laura stood watching until the last Indian disappeared over the horizon to the west.

Once the Indians had left, Ma and Pa were much happier. And when early spring had rolled around and the snow had thawed and green grass had sprouted everywhere, they were busier than ever. The first thing Pa did with the coming of spring was to hitch up the two horses and plow a patch of land for an early kitchen garden. When Pa was finished plowing, Ma hoed small holes in the turned sod, and Laura and Mary dropped in seeds and covered them with dirt. While they worked, baby Carrie sat at the edge of the garden, happily playing with a clump of grass.

"I can't wait to see the plants come up," Laura told her mother. And as she worked in the garden on that cloudless spring morning, there seemed no reason at all why Laura would not get her wish to watch the onions, peas, and carrots grow. But something very shocking was about to put all of the Ingalls family's hard work in jeopardy.

Chapter 3

Moving On

W hat do you mean?" Laura heard Pa say loudly. She turned from her job washing the dishes and crept to the open doorway of the cabin. Ma and Mary joined her there. They all peered out to see that Pa had stopped plowing and was talking animatedly to Mr. Scott.

"It's an outrage!" Charles Ingalls went on. "Why, if I'd known the politicians in Washington were going to draw the Indian territory line three miles east of here, I would never have settled on this land. To think they're going to send our own soldiers— American soldiers—to drive us off the land. Blasted politicians!"

Laura watched breathlessly. She had never seen her father so angry before.

Her mother stepped outside. "Hello, Mr. Scott," she said calmly. "Would you care for some poke-berry tea?"

"No, I best be on my way," Mr. Scott replied without looking directly at Ma. "Sorry about the bad news," he said to Pa. "You can read more about it in the newspaper if you want." Mr. Scott reached into his shirt and pulled out a newspaper, which he handed to Pa before strolling off.

Laura and Mary stood rooted at the doorway while, back in the cabin, Carrie stirred from her morning nap.

"What's the matter, Charles?" Ma asked.

"Well, you might as well know," Pa replied in a loud voice, not the usual voice he used when he wanted to talk privately to Ma. "We have to go. The politicians in Washington have decided that this is Indian territory, and they've sent soldiers to remove the white people from the land here."

"Are you sure we have to go?" Ma asked.

"Sure as I need to be," Laura heard him reply. "I'm not staying around here long enough to be driven off like a mangy dog."

Laura had no doubt that her father was seri-ous—his voice had an angry edge to it. She took a deep breath, stepped outside the cabin, and looked around. There was the well Pa had dug with his shovel, and the barn he'd built for the horses, the spring garden he'd planted, with the seeds tucked in the warm ground, and the straight rows for the corn that he had been plowing. Laura's father had been planning to harvest the corn when it was grown and take it to town to trade. As she looked around, Laura could not remember any other life than this, and she trembled at the thought of leaving the small cabin on the prairie.

True to his word, Charles Ingalls did not waste another minute plowing the land. He unhitched the horses from the plow and came right inside and started pulling the cupboards off the wall. "Might as well boil up all the potatoes, Caroline," he said as he worked. "No use saving them for seeding. I won't be doing any more planting."

At this Laura watched as her mother broke down in tears. "A whole year wasted!" Ma sobbed. "Just think of all that work, Charles."

Laura saw her father put his arm around her mother's shoulder. "Don't think about it that way," he said soothingly. "It's been a good year, and if we did this once, we can surely do it again somewhere else. What does a year amount to, anyway? We have all the time there is."

"Where will we go?" Ma asked.

"Well," Pa replied. "I've been thinking maybe we should head back to Wisconsin—to Lake Pepin."

Laura gasped with surprise. She had expected her father to go farther west to settle, but instead he had decided to go back to where she was born, back to her grandparents and aunts and uncles and cousins. Laura could not remember any of them, but she could imagine herself playing with other children her age!

Two days later, on a crisp April morning in 1871, four-year-old Laura Ingalls found herself sitting in a covered wagon—the same wagon that her family had traveled in from Wisconsin to Kansas. Her father had broken it down and stored it in the barn. As Pet and Patty clopped along, Laura stared out the back of the wagon, willing herself to recall every detail of the log cabin, the only home she had ever known. The place looked so lonely now, with its latch left open, ready for some wayfarers to take shelter in.

"Good-bye, little house," Laura whispered as the cabin shrank to a tiny spot on the horizon and then disappeared from view.

As the Ingalls family traveled toward the town of Independence, Kansas, they met up with other families along the way who had also made the decision to leave. There was a lot of head nodding and waving, but not much talking, as they fell into a line of wagons along the dusty track. Jack the dog, who was running alongside the wagon, did not even bother to bark at the other wagons.

By lunchtime they were approaching Independence. Pa told Laura that she had been to the town once before, but she could not remember it. As far as she was concerned, this was the first time she had ever visited a town, and she wondered what a real town would be like.

Laura peered out from the wagon as it rolled down the main street of Independence. The street was lined with single-story storefronts that housed such things as a bakery, a grocery store, a saddle maker, a furniture maker, a doctor, a bank, and various other businesses. Then, to her amazement,

Laura saw a two-story building. It was the first two-story structure she had ever seen, and she marveled at its size. It was so much bigger than the poky cabin she had called home for most of her short life.

In Independence Pa stopped long enough to trade the last few furs he had for provisions for the journey—corn, wheat flour, and bullets—and then they were off again. Laura watched as they passed a church and a store with a sign that read, "Verdigris Valley Drug Emporium." Laura had to ask her mother what the words said.

Ma read the words to Laura and then explained, "It's a store where you can buy paint, stationery, and fancy toys. Why, women can even buy perfume there."

Laura sat amazed as she watched Independence fade from view. So that's what a town is like, she thought to herself as the wagon wheels crunched along the dusty track.

That night the Ingalls family camped out under the stars northeast of Independence. A gentle breeze whispered through the tall prairie grass that surrounded them as Pa lifted the food box out of the wagon and Ma began preparing dinner. Laura and Mary were sent to gather twigs and sticks for the fire, and soon tiny sparks were drifting up into the evening sky, along with the smell of corn cakes. As Laura watched the cakes sizzling on the spider— the iron skillet with six short legs attached that lay over the fire—she thought about the adventures that lay ahead of them. Pa told her that it was nearly five hundred miles back to Lake Pepin in Wisconsin. This was a long way to travel, too long for Laura to take in, but she was sure there would be lots of exciting adventures.

The following morning everyone was up bright and early. Pa did not bother to light another fire. Instead everyone filled up on cold corn cakes that Ma had set aside from dinner the night before. Pa chugged some water from a big pottery jug, and then they all climbed back onto the wagon, and they were off on their way again.

They traveled alone, rarely seeing another wagon. And if a wagon did happen along, it was not headed north like they were, but west to the open frontier. When they crossed paths with another wagon, Pa would raise his hat and wish the settlers well. Other than that, days would pass before Laura would see another person. Only the wide, open, and empty prairie that stretched beyond the horizon kept the family company.

Despite being all alone on the endless prairie, Laura soon grew to love her days on the covered wagon. As long as Pa was sitting up front with his rifle slung across his knees and Jack was bounding alongside the wagon, she felt safe and happy.

Mary and Laura sat at the back of the wagon most of the time, while Ma, cradling baby Carrie in her arms, sat up front next to Pa. From their vantage point at the rear of the wagon, the girls could look back and watch for black, brooding clouds forming on the horizon. When such clouds came, Laura or Mary would crawl to the front and warn her father of the impending storm. Pa would bring Pet and Patty to a halt, climb down from the wagon, and roll down the canvas sides so that everything would stay dry inside. Then they would move on again.

When the first boom of thunder sounded, Ma would snuggle Carrie down beside the big girls. She would hold Laura's and Mary's hands while the storm passed over them. As long as they stayed in the middle of the wagon and did not brush against the canvas sides, they stayed dry. Pa, on the other hand, did not stay dry. He drove the wagon on through the rain, hunched over, water pouring off the brim of his hat and onto his buckskin jacket. "Great Jehoshaphat!" Laura would hear him exclaim with each crack of thunder.

Thankfully the storms usually disappeared as quickly as they appeared. And when they had passed, the girls were able to climb down from the wagon and run alongside it to stretch their legs. However, with each spring storm, the water level began to rise in the many creeks and rivers they had to cross on their journey. One of these crossings gave Laura a scare she would never forget.

The family had left Kansas behind and were making their way across Missouri when they came to a creek that they needed to ford. Laura heard Pa mumble something to Ma about how surprised he was at the level of water flowing in the creek. Laura looked at the water, which was brown and churning and flowing swiftly down the creek bed, carrying with it tree branches and other pieces of debris.

Laura watched as Pa walked along the edge of the creek bank on both sides of the wagon. Pa stopped every now and then to peer across at the far bank as well. Finally, he walked back to the wagon. "This is definitely the ford," he declared. "I can see old wagon tracks here and on the far bank. I think we'll be safe. I think we can make it across safely, Caroline."

"If you think so, Charles," Laura heard her mother reply.

With that, Pa swung back up onto the wagon and flicked the reins. Pet and Patty lurched forward, pulling the wagon into the fast-flowing creek.

"Lie down and be still," Ma ordered Mary and Laura.

The two girls quickly did as she said.

Laura felt the wheels bumping over stones in the creek bed, and then she felt something strange: the wheels were no longer bumping on the stones. Instead, the wagon seemed to rock gently from side to side.

"Take them, Caroline!" Laura heard her father say frantically. By the time she lifted her head to see what was happening, her mother was holding the reins and her father was gone. She crawled up onto her knees to get a better view. There was Pa, in the water with Pet and Patty. The surging water swirled around Pa, and Laura began to think she would never see him again, that he would be swept downstream and would drown. But Pa did not get swept away. He had somehow grasped Pet's bridle and seemed to be talking to the horses, though over the roar of the water Laura could not hear what he was saying.

The wagon rocked violently, and Laura was sure it was going to roll over. She felt a huge knot in her stomach and dived back onto the wagon floor beside Mary. It was then that she heard the thump of the front wheels. They had hit against something. Then she felt the rear wheels bang against something. It took Laura a few moments to realize that the wheels were once again rumbling over the stones at the bottom of the creek. Once again Laura scrambled to her knees, just in time to see Pa leading Pet and Patty out of the creek. They had made it safely across.

"That was close," Pa said when they were all finally safe on dry land. "I've never seen a creek come up so fast, right while we were in the middle of it. The wagon began to float, and the horses didn't know what to do. But they're good swimmers, and with a little encouragement I was able to get them to swim across the creek with the wagon behind. Good Pet, good Patty," he added, rubbing each horse's mane as he said it.

"Oh, Charles, I was so scared," Ma said.

"Me too," Laura added. "It's a good thing you knew what to do, Pa."

Although they were safe, fording the creek had taken its toll on everyone, and when the family came upon an empty cabin nearby, Ma and Pa stopped to look at it. The owner of the cabin came by and offered to let the family use it if Pa would help him make furniture for a week or two. A deal was soon struck, and Laura helped her parents and Mary unload the contents of the wagon into the cabin. The place was bigger than the cabin they had left in Kansas, but it was also a lot draftier. Still, Pa managed to get a good fire going in the fireplace, and soon they were all warm and dry.

Each morning Pa got up and went off to work while everyone else stayed behind. Ma was unsure of the area and would not let Mary and Laura wander too far into the nearby woods. Without being able to explore much, Laura found the days soon becoming monotonous. The highlight of the day was always when Pa arrived back and told them all about what he had been doing.

One windy day, when everyone was inside the house, Ma stopped darning one of Pa's shirts and said, "Listen, girls."

Laura and Mary stopped rethreading their Indian beads and listened. They could hear a crackling noise, quiet at first and then louder.

"Smoke!" Ma yelled. "I smell smoke. Laura, get Carrie, and you and Mary get outside now."

Laura scooped up her baby sister and headed along with Mary for the door. Outside she and Mary followed Ma around to the side of the cabin where flames were shooting up from the chimney.

"Stay here," Ma ordered the two older girls as she grabbed a bucket of water that was standing by the door and dashed back inside.

Laura ached to run back inside after her, but she knew that when her mother used that tone of voice, she expected complete obedience, and nothing less would do.

Finally the flames died down, and Ma reappeared at the door. "I think I put the fire out," she said, "but we'll stay outside for a while and watch the chimney to be sure." She handed the shawl she was carrying to Laura and Mary. "Here, you two, wrap yourselves up in this and keep warm."

The family had a lot to talk about that night, and when the candles were finally blown out, Laura heard her parents whispering to each other.

"I think we should leave here," she heard her mother say. "I just don't feel safe here all day without you around, Charles. The sooner we get back to Wisconsin, the better."

"I agree," her father replied. "I think I've made enough money to get us the rest of the way there, and Mr. Robinson has offered to trade Pet and Patty for two bigger horses. They've served us well, but they'll never pull the wagon up and down the Missouri hills."

Laura's heart lurched when she heard the news that Pet and Patty were leaving them. She knew it was no use begging Pa to let them stay. The horses were small, and Laura often felt sorry for them for the heavy load they had to pull across the prairie. As she drifted off to sleep, she thought of Pet and Patty trotting happily around a grassy field with no harnesses or bits in their mouths.

The next afternoon the Ingalls family were on their way northeast again. As they got closer to their destination, Laura asked many questions about her extended family. Her parents had rented out the cabin Pa had built near Lake Pepin before they moved to Kansas, and Uncle Henry and Aunt

Polly and their children lived in the cabin next door to it. The children, Louisa, Charles, Albert, Lottie, and Ruby, were what Ma called double cousins. This was because Ma's brother, Uncle Henry, had married Pa's sister, Polly.

Not only were Uncle Henry and Aunt Polly related on both sides of the family tree, but also Ma's younger sister Eliza had married Pa's older brother Peter, and they lived near Grandpa and Grandma Ingalls. Uncle Peter and Aunt Eliza Ingalls were the parents of four more double cousins— Alice, Ella, Peter, who was the same age as Laura, and a baby named Lansford, whom Ma had heard about when Pa brought back the mail from Independence the previous fall.

It was quite a lot for Laura to take in, especially since she could not recall meeting any of them. It was also a little unnerving to think that all of the adults there knew her but she did not know them.

It was mid-May when the weary Ingalls family finally arrived at Lake Pepin. Laura thought it was every bit as beautiful as Ma had described it, with towering oaks clothed in new green leaves lining the shoreline, and black-eyed Susans and other wild-flowers beginning to bloom everywhere she looked.

As they approached the end of their journey, Laura walked alongside the wagon, anxious to take in everything around her. There had been no way to get word to any of their relatives that they were coming, and she did not want to miss the expression on the face of anyone who recognized her ma and pa.

The horses clip-clopped their way through the tiny town of Pepin, with storefronts and houses lining the main street. Then Pa turned the wagon north beside Lost Creek, and the wagon rolled along the base of some bluffs. As the road eventually zigzagged its way up out of the ravine to the top of the bluff, it got steeper and steeper. Soon everything that was not tied down in the wagon slipped toward the back of it, and it was not long before Laura and Mary found themselves pinned to the backboard of the wagon.

"Hang on, girls," Pa yelled back to them, seeing their predicament. "We're nearly there."

And so they were. Just minutes later they were riding along the wooded bluff-top path. As they rounded a curve, Pa pulled on the reins, and the horses came to a halt. "We're home at last!" Pa whooped.

Laura climbed out of the wagon and took a cautious look at the little house in the big woods.

Chapter 4

A New Life in the Wisconsin Woods

The first thing Laura noticed about the house was that it was bigger than the cabin they had left in Kansas. It had a glass-pane window as well as a door in the front. All the way around the place ran a zigzagging split-rail fence to keep out the bears that Pa often talked about. Two enormous oak trees also stood guard in the front yard.

Two children soon ran out of the house, followed by a woman about Ma's age. Pa explained that this was the Gustafson family, who had rented the house when the Ingalls family had left for Kansas. Pa spoke to Mrs. Gustafson and told her that he and his family wanted to move back into the house as soon as she was able to arrange for somewhere else to live. Mrs. Gustafson said that that was fine because they were planning to head west soon anyway.

"Back in the wagon," Pa ordered Mary and Laura. "It's just a few turns up the road to Aunt Polly and Uncle Henry's house. They'll be surprised to see us!" Then he laughed the happy, carefree laugh that Laura loved to hear.

And what a welcome it was! As soon as they reached their destination, Laura was smothered with hugs until her ribs hurt. She could see that Uncle Henry looked like her ma and that Aunt Polly and her pa had the same bright blue eyes that she and Mary had. Then there were the cousins. At first Laura was a little shy to see so many other children in one place. Soon, though, she was jumping from stump to stump in the front yard with her older cousins Louisa, Charles, Albert, and Lottie while her younger cousins Ruby and a new baby, Lillian, sat and watched.

Before long the Gustafsons had moved out of the Ingallses' house, and Laura and her family moved back in. This was the house Laura was born in; Pa and Ma had built it with their own hands. Not only was it bigger than the cabin they had left in Kansas, but also it had three separate rooms. One was the main room, with a table, chairs, and woodstove in it. Next to the main room was Ma and Pa's bedroom, with a shuttered window. The three girls slept in the third room. This was the first time that Laura had not slept in the same room with her parents, and at first she felt a little frightened going to sleep.

The best thing of all about the house was the attic, which ran the length of the place. Laura had to climb a narrow ladder to get up to it. The ceiling was steeply sloped, and Laura had to reach up on tiptoes to touch the center of it. On rainy days there was no better place to play than in the attic.

"Now that we're settled, it's time to think about schooling," Ma told Mary one day, with Laura nearby. Laura's heart skipped a beat. Schooling—with shiny slates and rows of desks—was one of the things Laura longed for most.

"Mary, I have arranged for you to start school tomorrow. Cousin Louisa will come by and pick you up."

"And me?" Laura asked hopefully.

"You're only four," Ma replied. "There'll be plenty of time for you to go to school, and I need someone here to help me with Carrie and the chores."

Laura stood silent. She knew it was rude for children to talk back to their parents, but she desperately wanted to beg to be allowed to attend school with her big sister. It was a bitter moment the following morning as Laura watched her four Quiner cousins and her sister Mary disappear down the road toward Barry Corner, where the school was located. Laura was especially upset when she thought about her cousin Lottie, who was also only four years old and yet was able to go to school with the big children.

Ma kept Laura busy all day long, even lifting her up so that she could hang Carrie's newly washed baby gown on a tall bush. It was Monday, and Ma taught Laura a rhyme to remember what special chore had to be done each day of the week.

Wash on Monday
Iron on Tuesday

Mend on Wednesday
Churn on Thursday
Clean on Friday
Bake on Saturday
Rest on Sunday

But even reciting the rhyme could not stop Laura from thinking of all the fun Mary must be having at school.

By midafternoon Laura was standing at the gate, watching for her sister to appear. That night there was plenty to talk about as Pa sat by the fire, oiling the leather straps on his rabbit traps. Mary explained that there were nineteen children in school. The oldest boy was fifteen, and Lottie was the youngest. The school consisted of a single room, with the smallest children, including Lottie, sitting in the front row and the oldest students at the back. Mary also reported that her teacher was a kind woman named Miss Barry.

Laura noticed how Ma's eyes shined when Mary talked about the school. Ma had been a school-teacher herself a long time ago, when she was just sixteen, and Laura knew how important it was to her mother for her own children to be educated. "We can't have them running around the prairie without an ounce of schooling," she had often told Laura's father before they moved back to Wisconsin. All the conversation about learning made Laura want to go to school even more than ever, but she knew she would have to be patient.

Summer came, and with it the hottest weather that Laura could recall. Her petticoat prickled her legs, and her mother was constantly reminding her to wear her sunbonnet on her head, not tied around her neck and dangling down her back. Weeks passed without a drop of rain. Pa became anxious about fires breaking out, and Laura thought back to the chimney fire in the cabin they had stayed at in Missouri. Now Ma always kept a big bucket of water on the hearth when she was cooking. With the heat, dust seemed to find its way into everything, and the deer leapt through the forest, searching for water at dried-up creek beds. Pa began to be concerned that the wheat crop also would dry up. Laura was very grateful that her father had dug a deep well near the cabin, and people walking or riding by often stopped in for a scoop of the well's pure water.

In the evenings Ma would often read sections of the newspaper aloud to Pa as he cleaned his traps or made more lead bullets for the next day's hunting. In early October she read how in Chicago a cow had kicked over a lantern in a stable, starting a fire that leapt from the barn to the house, and then on to the next house, until much of the city was in flames. It was being called the Great Chicago Fire of 1871, and it had killed three hundred people and left over one hundred thousand people homeless. These numbers were so big that Laura could not grasp them. Just as bad, the same newspaper reported that hundreds of people had died in a fire in the town of Peshtigo on the other side of Wisconsin.

After reading such reports, Ma and Pa were anxious every time they smelled the slightest whiff of smoke in the wind. How Laura longed for the cool downpours they used to get on the Kansas prairie.

Not only did the showers cool things off, but also they dampened everything and took away the constant fear of fire.

During the long, hot summer, the Ingalls family made two trips, and Laura could not decide which one was more exciting. The first trip was a visit to her Grandma and Grandpa Ingalls, who lived thirteen miles north in the township of Rock Elm. Pa had hitched up the horses the night before and spread a blanket on the wagon seat for the girls to sit on. Then early the following morning everyone piled onto the wagon, and they were off. In the wagon was a big bundle of food that Ma had prepared for them to take. There were three loaves of bread, freshly churned butter, patted into Ma's special mold with a strawberry and two leaves on the bottom, smoked venison, and a blueberry pie. Laura wondered whether it was wrong to look forward to eating the pie almost as much as she looked forward to meeting her father's family.

The family arrived around midmorning at Grandpa and Grandma's house, where Laura met a dizzying array of relatives. Aunt Ruby was a teenager, and she lived at the house, as did Pa's younger brother George. Laura was amazed that Uncle George's eyes were exactly the same shade of blue as her father's. Just down the road lived Uncle Peter and Aunt Eliza and the double cousins, Alice, Ella, Peter, and Lansford. As if that were not enough new family members for Laura to be introduced to, her Uncle Hiram, Aunt Docia (who was Pa's sister), and the two Waldvogal cousins, Lena and Eugene, also lived nearby.

Grandpa Ingalls took Laura for a walk in the thick woods that surrounded the house. "These are maple trees," he said, pointing out the trees to Laura. "In late winter and early spring I drill small holes in the these trees and drain off some of their sap."

"Doesn't it hurt the tree?" Laura asked.

"No, child," Grandpa answered, "no more than it hurts you when you prick your finger."

They walked on a few more steps, and then Grandpa began explaining more of the process of collecting the sap. "The sap runs into a bucket, and I come by each day and collect it. I put the sap into a large cauldron over a fire and boil it for a long time. After it's boiled enough, I drain the sticky liquid into buckets to let it cool some. Then I boil the liquid some more, waiting for it to grain."

"What's graining, Grandpa?" Laura asked.

"That's when the liquid starts to crystallize, or turn to tiny grains. When it starts to do that, I put out the fire, and as fast as I can, I pour the graining syrup out into large milk pans, where the syrup turns into cakes of hard, brown maple sugar."

"I can hardly wait until I get to help you tap the maple trees, Grandpa," Laura said.

Grandpa chuckled. "Soon enough," he replied. But Laura hardly heard him; she was too busy thinking about the sweet maple sugar. She could almost taste it.

Laura loved everything about her grandparents' house. Their house was much larger than her house. The main room was long, with a kitchen and stove at one end and Grandma and Grandpa's bed at the other. In between was plenty of room for sliding along the floor. The boards were smooth and shiny and irresistible to Laura and to her cousin Peter, that is, until Ma gave Laura a raised-eyebrow look that told her she had better behave like a young lady.

All too quickly the visit was over, and before Laura knew it, Pa was lifting her back into the wagon, and they were off on their way home again.

A few days after the visit to Grandma and Grandpa Ingalls's house, Carrie turned one year old. Not long after Carrie's birthday, Laura made her second trip, this time to the town of Pepin, located seven miles southeast of the Ingallses' cabin in the woods. Once again Pa hitched up the horses to the wagon, and everyone climbed aboard for the journey. Mary and Laura sat on the seat their father had made for them by tying a board across the wagon box.

Laura could hardly believe it as they rolled along—they were going to town. Finally the road to town emerged from the woods and made its way along the edge of Lake Pepin. Pa explained that Lake Pepin was about thirty miles long and three miles across at its widest point and that it was, in fact, a part of the Mississippi River. When they rounded a bend in the road, Pa raised his arm and pointed. "There's Pepin, over there," he said.

Laura peered in the direction Pa was pointing. Sure enough, there was the town, nestled at the edge of the lake. Laura could make out one very large building close to the water and a number of smaller structures huddled together beyond it. As they got closer, Laura realized that most of the buildings in Pepin were constructed from milled planks of wood, not from logs, as with all the places she had lived.

When they got close to town, Pa pulled the horses to a halt, and they left the wagon by the lakeshore and walked the rest of the way. The big building Laura had seen from the distance was a general store, and Laura followed along as Pa and Ma led the way inside. Laura took two steps into the store and stood transfixed. There were so many interesting things packed into the place. Bolts of brightly patterned fabrics lined one side of the store. On the floor stood kegs of nails, lead shot, a new plow, and sacks of sugar, salt, and flour. Stacked on shelves on the other walls and hanging from the rafters was all manner of other items, such as saws, ax heads, hammers, shovels, cooking pots and plates, and knives and guns. But the thing that caught Laura's attention the most was the two large wooden pails full of candy. Laura stared longingly at the candy while Ma bought lengths of calico and denim cloth to make some new clothes for Pa.

Much to Laura's delight, when her parents had finished buying all the things they needed, the storekeeper reached into one of the pails of candy and handed a piece each to her and to Mary. The heart-shaped pieces of candy had red writing on them. Ma told Laura that the words on her piece of candy read "Sweets to the sweet." Laura giggled and popped the candy into her mouth and enjoyed its sweetness as it dissolved on her tongue.

The family walked back to the wagon at the lakeshore, where Pa lifted down the food box. Ma laid a blanket on the ground, and the family enjoyed a picnic of bread and butter, cheese, hard-boiled eggs, and cookies. After they had eaten, Pa walked back into town to talk to some of the men there while Laura and Mary played along the lakeshore.

It was late afternoon and the sun was casting long shadows across Lake Pepin when the Ingalls family set out for home again. By the time they got home, the sun had set and the moon had risen, bathing the surrounding landscape in a silver glow. When Laura finally climbed down from the wagon and walked inside, she could not imagine a better way to spend a day than making a trip to town.

Just as Ma was preparing to send Laura to school for the winter term, an unexpected setback took place. It happened less than a mile from the Ingallses' house, on the road to Barry Corner. A Swedish immigrant was hiking through the area, when two men attacked and robbed him. Worst of all, the incident occurred at three o'clock in the afternoon in broad daylight. That was right about the time that Laura and the others would be walking home from school when the new term started.

Laura knew that Ma would not want her to hear of such a horrible thing, but with so many cousins and playmates, news of the attack traveled fast. All the same, Laura tried to think about something else when she passed the spot on the road where it had happened, and she prayed that her mother would still let her walk that way to school when the time came. She was thankful that by the start of the winter term, Pa had convinced Ma that the robbers were long gone and that Laura could start her education.

In October the big day arrived. It was fall now, and Ma said that Laura could go to school until the snowdrifts got too deep for her to walk through them. Laura was delighted. Finally she was being allowed to go to school.

Laura quickly found school to be a fascinating place. For one thing, the schoolroom was the biggest room she had ever set foot in. And she recognized a number of the children in the room: her four cousins and Mary, of course, and one of her best friends, a five-year-old boy named Clarence Huleatts. The Huleattses lived nearby, and Clarence's parents and Laura's parents were good friends. Laura loved it when the two families got together because Clarence was a daredevil. He wore copper-toed shoes that did not scuff, and he liked to climb everything in sight.

Each morning Miss Barry would ring the school bell to signal the start of class. Laura was proud that she knew most of her letters, but it did not take long for her to realize that she had a lot of catching up to do. Reading was hard work! Still, by the end of the first week in class, she could sound out *cat, rat,* and *mat.* While this was good, it was also a little frustrating to Laura because she could not think of many important sounding sentences with *cat* and *rat* and *mat* in them.

"Keep working hard," Ma told Laura. "You'll be on the second spelling book in no time flat."

By the time December rolled around, Laura could read simple sentences, just as Ma had predicted. But by then she had something much more exciting to think about—her first Christmas with Grandma and Grandpa.

Chapter 5

A Christmas Surprise

Laura was nearly five years old now, and she knew all about Christmas. She could not really remember the previous Christmas, though Mary had told her of it many times. She especially liked hearing the part about how their neighbor had risked his life fording a swollen river to bring the girls presents. Laura still had the little tin cup she had found in her stocking from him, although the candy stick, the heart-shaped cake, and the shiny penny were long since gone, and she wondered what she would get for Christmas this year.

Finally it was Sunday, December 24, time to load up the sleigh and swish through the snow to Grandma and Grandpa's big house. Of all the ways to travel, Laura loved riding in the sleigh best of all. The family tucked themselves into it, engulfed in two huge buffalo skins, one under them and one serving as an enormous blanket over them. Laura's knitted scarf was wrapped around her head and mouth, leaving only a space for her eyes to see out. Pa cracked the reins, and they set off. Pa had attached sleigh bells to the horses' harnesses, and the bells jangled as the horses trotted along with the sleigh behind them.

To Laura everything around them was silvery white and magical. Icicles hung from the trees, through which a waxy sun peeked. Rocks and tree stumps had been turned into white mounds that dotted the way and showed Pa where the road was. As they slid along through the snow, Laura tried to count how many people would be at her grandparents' big house, but she lost count around twelve or thirteen.

The Ingalls family arrived at their destination just ahead of Uncle Henry and his family. Everyone piled into the house, where Grandma scooped up the children and stood them in front of the crackling fire. Laura spread her fingers and soaked up the warmth from the flames. Since it was Christmas, Grandma even handed each child a big, round molasses cookie to nibble on.

As the morning wore on, Ma, Grandma, and the aunts fussed around the stove, stirring baked beans, frying bacon, and checking on dried fruit pies baking in the oven. Wonderful smells drifted through the house, making Laura's mouth water. Before long the children, all ten of them, began to get restless indoors, and Laura's cousin Alice made a suggestion. "Let's go outside and make pictures."

Laura had no idea what Alice meant by this, but the rest of her cousins sounded eager to do it, so Laura put on her cape, mittens, and scarf and followed them outside.

Laura soon learned that making pictures meant climbing onto a tree stump, spreading your arms wide, and falling forward into the soft, powdery snow. The trick was then to push yourself up without disturbing the indentation you had made in the snow. If you did it properly, after you were standing up, there would be a perfect indentation, or picture, of you in the snow. It took a little practice at first, but before long Laura had mastered the art of getting up without disturbing the indentation, and soon she was leaving perfect pictures of herself in the snow. In fact, Laura was having so much fun that it seemed like hardly any time had passed before the door to the big house swung open and Ma called for her and Mary and the cousins to come inside and have lunch. Laura brushed the powdered snow off herself and trudged inside.

In the afternoon Pa, Uncle Henry, and Uncle Peter went out to chop down a Christmas tree. Grandma put a gold-painted star on top of the tree, and Ma organized the children to cut out paper dolls with which to decorate the tree. Of course they had to take turns with the scissors, but Laura did not mind; she was having so much fun looking around the room at the hubbub of activity that she didn't mind sharing the scissors.

Darkness descended early, as usual during the Wisconsin winter, and the extended family settled inside the house for the night. Pa pulled out his violin and played various songs that people requested. The tunes of "Horse Marines" and "My Darling Nellie Gray" were soon reverberating around the room.

As it grew late, Laura, Mary, Ella, and Alice all piled onto buffalo skins on the floor in a corner of the room near the fireplace, and Pa serenaded them to sleep with lullabies on his violin. Laura's last thoughts before falling asleep were of the Christmas tree and what might lie under it in the morning.

The next thing Laura knew, sunlight was glowing in through Grandma's calico curtains. It was Christmas morning! Laura wiggled around to find her slippers as Mary and then Ella woke up. She eagerly fingered her stocking by the fireplace while Ma set a big pot of water to boil on the stove so that the adults could enjoy a cup of coffee made with store-bought ground coffee.

With all her cousins finally awake and gathered around the fireplace, Laura asked, "Can we look inside, Pa? Santa Claus has been here; I can feel things in the bottom of my stocking."

Laura saw Ma and Pa grin at each other, and then Pa nodded. Immediately Laura thrust her hand into her Christmas stocking and pulled out a pair of bright red woolen mittens. She put them on and then took a deep sniff. The mittens smelled faintly of cloves, like the ones Aunt Polly hung in her kitchen. Laura looked around, and all of the children had the same mittens, the boys with a blue zigzag pattern around the cuffs and the girls with a white pattern.

"There's more!" Laura heard Peter exclaim, so she thrust her hand deeper into the stocking. This time she pulled out a long, flat stick of red-and-white peppermint candy. It was the exact same shade of red as her mittens, and she knew that she would always look at the mittens and think of this wonderful moment with the peppermint stick and her family around her at Christmas.

"Look under the tree," Ella gasped, and all eyes turned to the Christmas tree. Under it was a pile of presents, each present labeled with a name. Laura trembled with excitement. Surely there was a present under the tree just for her. She watched patiently as each present was metered out to the right person, who then opened it. Pa gave Ma a beautiful wooden shelf with ivy carved all around it, and Ma gave Pa a new blue vest she had made. Grandma got a calico apron, and Grandpa received a three-legged stool.

Then it was Laura's turn. Her present was about as big as her forearm and wrapped in brown paper. She pulled at the string around the package, and two black button eyes stared out at her. She had a doll at last! Carefully she picked it up and studied it. The doll was made of white cloth and was dressed in a pink-and-blue calico dress. Underneath the dress were red flannel stockings and black cloth shoes. The doll's face had been penciled in, and her cheeks and mouth were as red as pokeberries. Her hair was made of strands of black wool yarn. And, of course, her eyes were two black buttons. Laura was speechless with delight. Never in her wildest dreams had she imagined owning such a beautiful thing as this.

"Did you ever see such big eyes on a little girl!" Aunt Eliza exclaimed.

Suddenly Laura realized that the room was silent and everyone was looking at her. She giggled with joy. "I'm going to call her Charlotte," she announced.

The other children opened their presents, but Laura was not one bit jealous of what they received. As far as she was concerned, she had received the most wonderful gifts—a pair of red mittens, a peppermint candy stick, and, best of all, Charlotte.

It was hard to imagine that Christmas could bring any more joy, but the Christmas dinner that Grandma and the other women of the family prepared was the best food Laura had ever eaten. It was a feast of wonderful foods: salt-raised bread, Swedish crackers, baked beans, potatoes, bacon, and dried pokeberry and apple pies and a big jar of molasses cookies to finish off the meal.

When dinner was finally over, no one felt much like moving. "Tell us a story, Grandpa, about when you were a boy," Alice begged, and soon all of the children were pestering Lansford Ingalls for a story. Laura settled down on the buffalo skin on the floor beside Mary and listened as her grandfather began his story.

"Things were a little different when I was a boy," Grandpa started as he rocked gently in his chair. "Take Sunday, for instance. Sunday was yesterday, and we were busy getting everything ready for today,

Christmas Day. When I was a boy that would never be. You see, we had to keep the Sabbath, as Sunday was called. And the Sabbath didn't begin when the sun came up on Sunday morning, but it began when it went down on Saturday night, and it lasted until the sun went down on Sunday. And when the sun went down on Saturday, you had to stop whatever work or play you were doing and stay solemn and respectful for all the next day. We couldn't laugh or poke each other or play jokes on each other. We had to put on our best clothes and go to church, and read catechism in the afternoon. And we had to walk to church, no matter what the weather, 'cause hitching the horses to the wagon for the trip was considered work, and you couldn't work on the Sabbath. Why, we even had to eat cold food my ma cooked the day before because cooking was considered working on the Sabbath as well."

As she listened to Grandpa speak, Laura was glad she was alive today, because keeping the Sabbath like Grandpa had to did not sound like much fun.

"Anyway, my two brothers, James and George, and I had built ourselves a wonderful sled. You see, our house was located along a road halfway up a steep hill, and we were going to use the sled to ride down from the top of the hill to the bottom. We planned to try out the sled on Saturday afternoon, because that was when we got to play. But Pa had kept us busy with chores all day, and before we could pull the sled to the top of the hill and slide down, the sun had set and it was the Sabbath. Of course we were disappointed, but there wasn't much we could do about it.

"So the next morning we went to church and then came home and had our cold lunch. Then, like always, me and my brothers sat down next to each other on a bench to read our catechism while Pa sat in his chair on the other side of the room, reading his Bible. And that was how we were supposed to pass the afternoon until the sun went down.

"After about an hour we heard snoring coming from Pa. James and George looked at each other, and first one and then the other tiptoed out of the room. I was the youngest, and at first I wasn't sure what to do, but then I got up and tiptoed out as well. Outside, my brothers were already pulling the sled to the top of the hill, and I ran to catch up to them. At the top we turned the sled around and prepared to ride down the hill. James sat in front, and George and I sat behind him. I sat at the back 'cause I was the smallest. And then we were off down the hill. We had to be quiet no matter how exciting it was so we wouldn't wake Pa."

Suddenly Laura's concentration was broken when her sister Carrie, now a toddler, walked over and plopped down in her lap. Laura wrapped her arms around Carrie and turned her attention back to Grandpa and his story.

"The sled began to go faster and faster," Grandpa was saying, "and it was very exciting. But then, as we approached the house, what should appear but a big, black pig! He walked out of the woods and stood right in our way. We were going too fast to stop, and suddenly the sled went right under the pig's belly, tipping him off his feet and into James's lap. Now we were three brothers and a pig racing down the hill."

The children laughed, and Grandpa carried on.

"The trouble was, the pig squealed with fright as loud as it could and would not stop. It was enough to wake the dead, and certainly enough to wake Pa. He was standing in the doorway watching us as we raced past the house. That pig did not stop fussing and squealing until the sled stopped at the bottom of the hill, when it jumped out of James's lap and ran back into the woods.

"I looked at James and George. No one said a thing. We just wondered what Pa was going to do to us for breaking the Sabbath. We trudged back up the hill, left the sled out back, and went inside. Pa was back in his chair, reading his Bible. He looked up but didn't say a word when we walked in. Quickly we took our places on the bench and went back to reading our catechism. Pa's reaction was a surprise to me: he just sat there reading. But when the sun set and the Sabbath was over, he took each of us out to the woodshed and laid a whipping on us for what we did. Why, my behind still stings just thinking about it after all these years."

Again the children laughed, and again Laura reminded herself how lucky she was to be alive today and not when Grandpa was a boy.

The following day it was time for everyone to head home, and Laura tucked Charlotte into the sleigh beside her. She could still hardly believe how lucky she was to have a new doll.

"See you soon. Hope we get a sugar snow this year," Laura heard her father yell as the horses turned toward home.

"Pa, what's a sugar snow?" Laura asked.

"Well, Half Pint," Pa began, "when we have a late snow in early spring, the cold holds back the leafing of the trees, causing the sap to run longer. And if the sap runs longer, it means that your Grandpa can collect more sap and make more maple sugar, enough for Grandma to cook with all year long. And best of all, Grandma and Grandpa always throw a big party when there's a sugar snow. All the neighbors come and dance into the night."

"Where?" Laura asked.

"In their house," Pa replied. "They push the bed back against the wall and make room. If I'm home, I play the fiddle, and your ma is the finest looking woman there, in her green dancing dress."

"Oh, Charles," Ma said. "I might look nice in my dress, but your ma is the best dancer by far."

Pa laughed. "Well, you might be right there, Caroline. Laura Ingalls has the nimblest feet in the township."

Laura smiled to herself. She liked the idea that she had been named after such a nice person as her grandma—and such a good dancer too.

"I sure hope there's a sugar snow this year," Laura said.

Soon after Laura and her family arrived home, a blizzard struck, and mountains of snow fell throughout the area. The snow covered the walls up past the windows, and Pa had to shovel it away from the door four or five times a day so that they were not snowed in. Laura did not mind this at all. She loved the feeling of being snuggled up inside while a white blanket covered everything around her. Besides, she had Charlotte to play with, and Ma let the children use the attic as their playroom. Laura and Mary turned a huge orange pumpkin stored in the attic into a table, and two smaller pumpkins became chairs. Piles of walnuts, hickory nuts, and hazelnuts were also stored in the attic, and they became make-believe food. The two girls had saved acorns and made them into little cups for their dolls. Smoked venison hung from the rafters on hooks, and the girls were allowed to use the hooks to hang quilts to create "rooms" in their pretend house.

Because it was too cold and snowy to go to school, Ma made Mary and Laura do some school-work, and she also started both Mary and Laura on making a simple nine-square quilt. Mary loved the meticulous work of piecing the bits of used cloth together so that the fabric had no puckers and the stitches were perfectly straight and even, but Laura found every stitch a chore. She begged her mother to let her stop, but Ma reminded her that one day she would be a mother and would need to make all of the clothes for her children. Laura knew that there was no way around it but to try her best, even though she was sure that her quilt would never be anywhere near as good as her big sister's.

Finally spring approached, and the snow began to melt. Icicles as thick as Laura's leg dropped off the eaves of the cabin, and the streams swelled with the spring thaw. Then, just as Pa was giving up hope, the family awoke one morning to a fresh blanket of snow. Everyone peered out the window at it. "Yes," Pa confirmed as they looked, "this is a sugar snow."

Laura clapped her hands with delight. "That means Grandpa and the uncles can make more sugar."

"You're right, Half Pint," Pa said, patting Laura on the head. "By my count, Grandpa should be sugaring off next Monday, and we'll all go over there, and maybe you can help Grandma bake some cookies."

"And don't forget about the dance," Mary interjected.

A thousand questions ran through Laura's head. Who would be at the dance? Would she be allowed to help Grandpa tap the sap? What was Ma bringing to help with supper? And how long would they be allowed to stay up and watch the grownups? But Laura knew that her mother thought it was bad manners for a child to ask too many questions, so she hugged Charlotte tightly and waited anxiously for sugaring-off Monday to arrive.

Chapter 6

A Sugar Snow

The Ingalls family were up before the sun on Monday morning. They ate a hearty breakfast, and then while Ma washed the dishes, Mary and Laura made their beds by lamplight. Then it was time to climb into the sleigh for the thirteen-mile trip to Grandma and Grandpa's house. They were well on their way when the sun finally climbed into the chilly morning sky, revealing wisps of mists threaded around the trees in the woods. Now that the darkness was gone and they could see, Pa began to point out the various animal tracks in the snow as they passed them in the sleigh.

"See those little tracks over there, Half Pint?" he said, pointing. "They belong to a cottontail rabbit. And those funny tracks are made by snowbirds. And those there, they are fox tracks."

Laura looked at all the various tracks Pa was pointing out and marveled at how he knew what animal they belonged to. Pa sure did know the woods well.

Finally, with the sleigh bells jangling, the horses pulled to a halt in front of Grandma and Grandpa's house. Grandma came to the door and beckoned them all to come inside. Laura and Mary scrambled out of the sleigh and ran inside to stand by the fire while Ma carried Carrie into the house.

When Pa learned that Grandpa and Uncle George were already out collecting sap from the maple trees and were preparing to start the fire to get the boiling process under way, he left the women at the house and headed out into the woods to help. Then the women got to work cooking. Grandma, Ma, and Aunt Ruby all pitched in preparing pies, cakes, and cookies to eat at the dance that evening. Laura watched them work. It all smelled so good, and she could hardly wait for the party to roll around when they would get to eat all the wonderful food that was being cooked.

The men had taken their lunch with them out to the woods, so Ma made cold venison sandwiches for Laura and Mary and Grandma and Aunt Ruby to eat. They all ate the sandwiches as they sat around the dining table, and then the women got back to work.

Following lunch Grandma put a pot of water on the cookstove to boil. She added some salt, and when the water began to boil, she sifted cornmeal into the pot with one hand while using a large wooden spoon to stir it with the other.

Laura was intrigued. "What are you making?" she finally asked.

"Why, I'm making hasty pudding," Grandma replied. "We'll eat it for supper with some of the maple syrup the men are boiling up out in the woods."

Maple syrup! Laura could hardly wait for supper.

Late in the afternoon, as the sun was sinking toward the horizon, Pa and Grandpa arrived at the house. Around their necks were wooden yokes, and from either side of each yoke hung a wooden bucket filled with hot maple syrup. Grandma placed a huge kettle on the cookstove, and the men poured their buckets of syrup into the kettle. Soon Uncle George arrived from the woods. He too was carrying a bucket of hot syrup, which he poured into the kettle.

Grandma then scooped servings of hasty pudding onto plates, and Ma ladled maple syrup over the pudding, and then everyone ate supper. The pudding and maple syrup tasted so sweet and delicious to Laura, and she was still savoring the taste when Uncle George suddenly leapt up from the table, grabbed his bugle, and headed out the door. Moments later he began blowing the bugle as loud as he could, and the horn's sound reverberated through the woods. (Pa had told Laura that during the Civil War Uncle George was a bugler in the army, where he had learned to play the instrument.)

"That should let 'em know it's time to get ready and head on over," Uncle George said when he came back inside.

"Then I guess we all better get ourselves ready," Grandma said, pushing herself away from the table.

Soon the house was a hive of activity. Ma and Grandma cleared away the dishes and washed them. They then swept the hearth and the floor. The table was pushed back against the wall, and the pies, cakes, and cookies baked earlier in the day were laid out on it, along with bread, cold pork, and pickles.

While Ma and Grandma worked, Laura watched Aunt Ruby get ready for the dance. Aunt Ruby washed and brushed her long hair until it was soft and shining, and then she laced up her corset and put on a pretty dress. Laura was amazed how beautiful she looked. Aunt Ruby had the same golden-colored hair as Mary and Carrie, leaving Laura as the only one with mousy brown hair.

Ma looked beautiful as well. With the work done, she had changed into a dark-green dress made of delaine, a worsted wool fabric.

With everybody ready, people began to arrive at the house. Some arrived on foot, having walked through the woods, while others arrived in sleighs and on wagons. Many of the women carried babies, and when they wanted to dance, they would lay their babies down on Grandma and Grandpa's big bed.

Soon the big house was filled with people: women in swirling dresses, men in boots, coats, and hats, and children watching from the corners of the room.

Laura watched Pa pull out his fiddle, tune it, and then begin to play. As he played, the adults formed into two circles in the middle of the room, the women forming the inside circle and the men the outside one. The circle of men then moved one way while the women went the other way. Pa announced to everyone what to do as he played. "Grand right and left," he said, raising his voice above the fiddle. And then, "Swing your partner."

At this, each man bowed to the woman on his left and then took her by the arm and swung her around.

Laura was entranced with the dancing. The women looked so beautiful and light on their feet as they moved across the dance floor. And everyone seemed to be having so much fun. Then Uncle George grabbed Laura by the hand and led her onto the dance floor. Soon Laura was dancing and twirling with everyone else.

Pa played and called several dances, and then the adults took a break from dancing. Several of the women went over to the kitchen, where Grandma was still hunched over the huge kettle, stirring the boiling maple syrup. She had been there the whole time that everyone else was dancing. Laura watched as the women took the big wooden spoon out of Grandma's hand and led her into the middle of the large room. Pa then began to play his fiddle again, and Uncle George jumped up to dance.

Laura recognized the tune her father was playing on the fiddle: "The Arkansas Traveler." As Pa played, the adults formed a circle and clapped in time to the music, with Uncle George in the middle, doing a jig. Then Grandma stepped forward. Uncle George bowed to her, and the two of them began to do a jig.

Laura burrowed her way to the edge of the circle to get a better view. Her grandma sure could dance. She moved as though her body weighed nothing at all. Uncle George, on the other hand, was huffing and breathing deeply as he danced, and beads of sweat glistened on his forehead. The couple danced and danced. And when Pa upped the tempo of the song, they danced harder and faster while the people clapped and cheered them on. By now the beads of sweat were running down Uncle George's face and dripping onto his coat. He seemed to be breathing heavier than ever, while Grandma just kept dancing, matching her son's every move.

Finally Uncle George could jig no more. He bowed to Grandma and left the circle. But Pa kept playing, and Grandma kept dancing until the song was over, and then everyone applauded her.

No sooner had Grandma finished dancing than she escaped back to the kitchen, where she took up her wooden spoon and began stirring the maple syrup again. It wasn't long before she announced to everyone, "The syrup is waxing. Come help yourselves."

People headed toward the kitchen, and Laura followed right along. Like everyone else, she took a plate and walked outside into the cold night, where she piled her plate with fresh white snow. After everyone went back inside, Grandma ladled maple syrup over each plate of snow. Immediately the coldness of the snow turned the syrup into soft maple candy, and Laura, along with the others, enjoyed every mouthful of the sweet concoction.

The guests at the dance then moved to the table and began to eat the food laid out there. Laura ate a slice of pie and a cookie, which tasted even better than they had smelled while they were baking earlier in the day.

When people had finished eating, Pa picked up his fiddle again and struck up another tune. Once again the adults began to dance. Laura watched from the side of the room as Grandpa swirled Ma around and around.

Suddenly Laura's eyes began to feel heavy, and she could hardly keep them open. The next thing she knew, it was morning, and she woke up lying across the foot of Grandma's bed, in which Ma, Grandma, and Carrie were sleeping. She popped her head up and saw that Pa and Grandpa were sleeping on the floor in front of the fireplace, with several blankets draped over them. Meanwhile Mary was asleep tucked in beside Aunt Ruby in her bed.

Before long everyone was awake. Pa stoked the fire while Grandma and Ma headed to the kitchen. Ma loaded wood into the cookstove while Grandma mixed batter. When the fire in the stove was roaring, Grandma placed a skillet on top of the stove and began making pancakes. Laura's mouth watered as she breathed in the wonderful smell, and it wasn't long before she was sitting at the table, eating pancakes with maple syrup for breakfast.

After breakfast it was time to head back home.
Pa hitched the horses to the sleigh, and Uncle
George lifted first Laura and then Mary into the
sleigh. After everyone had said good-bye, Pa cracked
the reins, and they were off. As they rode along,
Laura thought about how wonderful the day at her
grandparents' house had been, especially the
dance. She decided that it had been the best day of
her life, and she would never forget it.

Once the sugar-snow melted, spring arrived in
Wisconsin, carpeting the meadows with wildflowers
and filling the fruit trees with blossoms. Laura was
five years old, and as long as she promised to stick
close to Mary and obey her, the two girls were
allowed to walk farther afield—down the hill to a
friend's house or through the woods to Uncle Henry
and Aunt Polly's.

With winter over, school started up again, and
Laura was proud to be promoted to the second
spelling book and to be now sitting partway back in
the schoolhouse room.

The summer of 1872 brought with it lots of
exciting events, including another trip to Pepin,
more visits to Grandma and Grandpa's house, and
long days playing with various cousins. When she
had nothing else to do, Laura would watch Pa prepare the wheat field for planting. First he plowed it,
making long furrows in the ground, and then in the
furrows he planted wheat seeds. Slowly the wheat
sprouted and pushed up through the ground and
began to grow. Soon the field was a sea of gold that
moved gently back and forth in the wispy summer

breeze. Finally Pa harvested the wheat, tying the harvested stalks into large bundles and stacking them at the end of the field.

Then one day, soon after Pa had harvested the wheat, Uncle Henry brought the wheat he had harvested from his field and stacked the bundles beside Pa's. Intrigued, Laura asked Pa, "Why'd Uncle Henry bring over his wheat and leave it in the field with yours?"

"Ah, Half Pint, it won't be long now and you'll see why," Pa replied.

Sure enough, not long afterward, as summer began to give way to fall, two men with a strange machine pulled by four horses came up the road past the cabin and headed out to the wheat field. Pa took his two horses and headed to the field as well.

After they had finished their chores around the house, Laura and Mary ran out to the wheat field to see what was going on. They arrived there at the same time as Uncle Henry, who was leading his two horses behind him. The two men and Pa had already set up the machine. It was unlike anything Laura had ever seen. One part of it was like a long wooden table that had a funny canopy over the middle of it. A long, wide leather belt seemed to wrap right around the table longways, and a big wheel with teeth on it protruded from the side of the machine. But it was the other piece of equipment that really fascinated Laura. A long iron rod stretched from the table-like contraption to what looked something like an upturned wagon wheel. The rod had two small wheels with teeth at either end. One end interlocked with the big wheel on the table, and the other end interlocked with teeth on the bottom of the wheel-like machine. Four long poles reached out from the center of the wheel. Laura watched as Pa and Uncle Henry hitched up their horses along with the four horses that had been pulling the machine. Soon two horses were hitched to the end of each of the four poles.

"Pa, what is this?" Laura asked.

"This here is a threshing machine. That's a separator," Pa said, pointing to the table-like contraption. "It's going to separate the grains of wheat from the stalks. And that there, that machine's called a horsepower. And since it has eight horses attached to it, it's an eight-horsepower machine. And that rod, it's called the tumbling rod. As the horses walk around and around, they turn the tumbling rod, which drives the machine. You and Mary stand back now and watch how it all works."

And that is what they did. A man with a whip sat on a stool on top of the wheel, and soon he had the horses walking round and round in a circle. Sure enough, the tumbling rod began to turn, and the separator started to make a loud noise, and the wide leather belt began to move round and round. Soon Pa and Uncle Henry were taking the bundles of wheat they had harvested one by one, cutting the thin rope that bound them, and placing the stalks onto the belt. The stalks were carried along the belt and under the canopy over the middle. Then, to Laura's amazement, grains of wheat began to pour out of a shoot on the side of the separator while the remainder of the stalks were carried on along the belt and dropped off the end into a big pile. A man collected the grain pouring out into buckets and tipped the full buckets into sacks. He had to work hard and fast because by the time he had emptied one full bucket by tipping its contents into a sack, he had to quickly grab another bucket before it overflowed.

It took several hours until all the wheat was threshed, and then Pa and Uncle Henry helped the two men pack up the machine. When they were done, several sacks of wheat—payment for the use of the thresher—were loaded onto the back of the wagon, and the two men and their machine were off.

When they were gone, Laura watched as Pa turned to Uncle Henry and said, "That machine sure is a great invention. It would have taken you and me at least two weeks apiece to thresh that much wheat. And even then, we wouldn't have gotten as much wheat as that machine was able to thresh."

Uncle Henry nodded in agreement.

In the fall Pa hunted and trapped, but he often lamented that it was becoming increasingly difficult to find deer and bears, as more and more settlers were moving into the area. When Pa complained, Laura would often catch a glimpse of her mother raising her eyebrows and shaking her head a little. Laura knew that her father was the one with "wandering feet" and that her mother preferred to live in "civilization."

During the fall of 1872 and on through winter and then into spring of 1873 and into summer, Pa brought up the idea of going west. He and Ma began to have serious discussions around the fire at night. Their discussions always took place when the three girls were tucked into their beds, but Laura often strained to hear what they were saying.

"I'm a frontiersman, Caroline," she heard her father say, "not a farmer. A field of wheat is not nearly as exciting to me as a well-stocked forest. I need places to roam and the smell of the open prairie."

Laura found herself rooting for her father. The wide-open spaces beckoned her just as much as they did him.

Finally, in September 1873, Pa announced that he had sold the house and land in the Wisconsin woods and that the family would be moving into Uncle Peter's house for the winter. At the first sign of spring—but before the ice melted on Lake Pepin—Uncle Peter and his family, along with Ma, Pa, Mary, Laura, and Carrie, would all head west into Minnesota.

Laura leapt about the house when she heard the news. But then, as she helped her mother pack up their belongings and load them into the wagon, she began to think of all the things she would miss about living in the big woods. Her friends were here, as well as her neighbors and her many cousins, aunts, and uncles whom she would not see again for a long time. She wondered whether she would ever go to school again or see her grandparents before they died. These were new and sobering thoughts for Laura, and she did not like them.

The months passed quickly at Uncle Peter's house, and Laura spent a lot of time helping Aunt Eliza care for two-year-old Lansford. Then, not long before her seventh birthday, Laura felt itchy and cranky. Mary, Carrie, and the four cousins living in the house all seemed out of sorts as well, and soon everyone could see why. Each of the children had a bright red rash and a rocketing temperature. Aunt Eliza pronounced the diagnosis—scarlet fever.

Every time Laura tried to sit up, her head thumped, yet every bone in her body ached when she lay down. Sweat soaked through the sheets and into the ticking of the mattress, and Laura wished someone would open the windows and let the frigid air inside. She was vaguely aware that all the other children were also sick and that their parents hovered over them all, alternately praying for them and offering them tin cups filled with cold water.

Laura was the first to recover from the scarlet fever, though she was weak for several weeks afterward. Thankfully no one died from the often-fatal disease, and everyone finally made a full recovery.

By the time the children were up and running around again, it was time to load the wagons. This was a thrilling moment for Laura, especially since she would be travelling with her cousins. Laura always thought that boys got to have more fun than girls, so she intended to stick close to her cousin Peter.

It was sad to say good-bye to Grandma and Grandpa. Laura had grown to love them and would miss them. Tears rolled down her cheeks as she hugged them one last time. It was also difficult to say good-bye to her aunts and uncles and cousins who were staying in Wisconsin.

Finally the day of departure arrived, and the two wagons lumbered off down the still-snow-covered road toward Pepin. The wagon wheels slipped and slid as they went down the icy hills, but finally the town of Pepin appeared on the horizon. Laura marveled at how different the place looked in the winter. Snow covered the streets, and the trees along the lake edge that provided refreshing shade in the summer stood bare and exposed.

Pa and Uncle Peter pulled the wagons to a halt and then stood up on their seats and peered out over the lake, looking for signs of cracks in the ice.

"Looks like we are in time. We should make it across," Pa said.

"Yep," Uncle Peter agreed, "but I wouldn't want to wait any longer."

Laura looked at Mary and knew she was thinking the same thought: What if the ice didn't hold? She recalled the horrible experience in Missouri on their way back to Wisconsin from Kansas when their wagon was nearly swept away crossing a swollen river.

Still, there was nothing that Laura could do but hold on tight to the side of the wagon as Pa maneuvered it over the snowy shoreline and out onto the ice. Somewhere on the other side of Lake Pepin was Lake City, Minnesota, and, Laura hoped, a great adventure beyond.

Chapter 7

On the Banks
of Plum Creek

W e made it!" Uncle Peter yelled as he guided his wagon off the ice and across the mushy snow of the lakeshore. Laura let out a long sigh of relief when she finally felt the wheels of the wagon bite into the dirt. They were on dry land again. The first part of their journey was over.

The two families spent the next three days staying in a cheap hotel in Lake City, Minnesota, on the other side of Lake Pepin. Ma took the opportunity to show the girls the city library, which contained newspapers and magazines from all over the country. Laura noticed that her mother stood for a long time in front of the list of monthly lectures. If there was one thing Ma liked, it was reading books and learning about new things.

The day before they were due to continue their journey west was Laura's seventh birthday. Pa gave Laura a small book of poetry called *The Flowret*. Some of the words in the book were too hard for Laura to read, but as Ma pointed out, a little more schooling would turn that around. Mary promised to read a poem to Laura every morning until both girls had memorized them all.

The following morning the two families set out again. The Ingalls family had never traveled in such cold weather before; it was still only February. Pa and Uncle Peter had set out early because they needed to make it across Lake Pepin while the lake was still iced over. But since it was so early, snow still lay on the ground, making the going hard for the wagons and horses. The wagon wheels slipped on the hills, and sometimes it was impossible to find the road because it was shrouded in new snow.

A week after setting out from Lake City, they were all relieved when they found an empty house beside a creek. The water in the creek was running, and Pa announced that they would all be staying in the house until the spring thaw set in. Laura had never felt happier than she did when she stood beside the roaring fire in the house, warming her hands while Ma stirred a huge pot of cornmeal. She had nothing to do but wait and play with her cousins until the men decided that conditions were right for them to be on their way again. The only thing that clouded Laura's happiness as she waited was learning that Uncle Peter, Aunt Eliza, and her cousins were not going to continue the journey to western Minnesota. Instead Uncle Peter had decided to stay in the area and had rented a farm near the house they were taking shelter in.

As much as Laura hated to be separated from Uncle Peter, Aunt Eliza, and her cousins, she was glad that her ma and pa had not decided to settle nearby. She wanted to go farther west as much as Pa did. When the spring thaw came, the two families parted company, and once again it was just Pa, Ma, Mary, Laura, and Carrie bumping along in the wagon laden with everything the family owned.

So many things along the way on the trip west delighted Laura, but the thing that startled her most was a long, haunting wail she heard late one afternoon. At first she thought it was a moose call, but her father laughed. "Why, Laura, that's a train whistle. We're near the railroad tracks. Look east, and you might see the smoke of the engine."

Sure enough, as Laura stood up on the wagon seat, she could see a puff of white smoke in the distance. She heard another whistle, and then a steam locomotive towing a line of carriages came into view. Carrie joined Laura on the seat, and the whole family stood spellbound as the train hissed and clanged its way past them. The wagon was close enough to the train tracks that Laura could see passengers sitting inside lighted carriages. Some were eating, while others looked out the window at her. She waved to the engineer, who in turn pulled on the whistle for her.

"It's a great age we live in," Pa told Laura after the train had passed. "Before I'm gone, railroads will have conquered the frontier."

That night, and for many nights afterward, Laura would lie awake thinking about the train. Where was it going? Who was traveling on it? What kind of adventures were the travelers off to find?

The Ingalls family traveled on, leaving the railroad tracks behind and heading out across the prairie. They crossed Sleepy Eye Creek and then the Cottonwood River. Then, long after the trail had ended, they came to a halt outside a small house that stood alone on a flat, grassy plateau above a creek. Pa swung himself down from the wagon and knocked on the door of the house. A young man emerged, followed soon afterward by a woman holding a baby. Pa talked quietly to the couple for a few minutes and then turned, smiling from ear to ear.

"Great news!" Pa said. "Mr. Nelson here says that there is a settler nearby who wants to sell up and move west. What do you say, Caroline? Do you think you could learn to love a place like this?"

Laura looked around with renewed interest. "What's the name of the creek?" she asked Mr. Nelson.

"Plum Creek, on account of the wild plums that grow along it in the fall," he replied.

"Plum Creek," Laura repeated, thinking it had a nice ring to it. She imagined herself in a house like Mr. Nelson's, with its store-bought windows and smooth machine-cut door. A quarter of an hour later, Pa stopped the wagon on a hill. "This is it, I guess," he said, with a twinkle in his eye.

"But, Pa," Laura interjected, "there's no house here."

"Looks can deceive you," he laughed.

Just then a man appeared from around the side of the rise and waved a greeting. Pa helped everyone down from the wagon and then shook hands with the man. His name was Mr. Hanson, and he was indeed planning on selling up and heading farther west.

Still puzzled as to where the house was, Laura took Carrie's hand and followed the two men down the incline toward Plum Creek. Suddenly they were all standing in front of a wooden door that opened into a hole in the creek bank.

Laura gasped. She had once seen a picture in a book of fairytales of a gnome who lived in a hole in the ground like this.

"It's not much, but it's warm in winter and big enough for a family," Mr. Hanson said. "And I'd be willing to trade it for your wagon and horses."

Half an hour later the deal was done, and the Ingalls family had a new home underground, 172 acres of rich prairie land, and two oxen, while Mr. Hanson had a wagon, along with two horses, to take his family farther west. Laura was not quite sure how she felt about it all as she spent her last night camping out in the open. Part of her wished that she were going farther west with the Hansons. It seemed a pity to end their adventure and move into a dirt house. But at least now, she comforted herself, she would know how rabbits and moles felt living in holes.

The following morning the Ingallses' possessions were unloaded from the wagon and were replaced by the Hansons'. By lunchtime Laura was watching the wagon lumber off across the prairie, ready to continue its adventure with another family. Pa had to travel as far as the nearest town with the Hansons so that all the paperwork changing the ownership of the land to him could be completed and the deal made official.

The reality of their new living situation settled on Laura as she helped Ma bring the bedding inside. Their new home was called a sod house. A cave had been dug into the creek bank, and the front of it had been covered with sod. Now that it was spring, the grass on the outside had grown green and thick, and the only thing that gave away the fact that a house was there was the door. Inside, the earthen walls had been compacted, and Laura could even trace tree roots running around them. Ma assured Laura that they would whitewash the walls as soon as they had settled in.

Pa arrived back from town early in the evening. Two days later he asked Laura and Mary if they wanted to walk to town with him. The town was called Walnut Grove, and it lay two miles south of them across the open prairie. Both girls jumped at the chance to see the place, and Ma let them wear their Sunday ribbons in their braids. Everything about that day delighted Laura. She loved walking across the prairie, which was thick with white daisies with glowing golden centers.

When they reached the first houses of Walnut Grove, Pa explained that the town had been laid out only a month before. Walnut Grove was a depot stop on the new railroad that had pushed into the area the previous fall. Twenty-four blocks had been surveyed, three in one direction and eight in the other. New buildings were going up everywhere, and Laura tried to imagine what they might look like when they were finished. As she walked along the newly surveyed streets, Laura heard many foreign languages and accents, and Pa told her that the new township had attracted people from Scotland, Norway, Sweden, and Ireland. Sometimes Laura's heart skipped a beat when she saw children her own age. Perhaps she would be able to go to school with them soon.

The town had one general store, right in the center of town, and Laura trailed her father inside. She was soon absorbed with the variety of goods available for sale: patterned calicos, laces, and nearly a dozen different sorts of candies. Her father told her that the goods in the store had come by train directly from Minneapolis and Chicago. Before they left the store, Laura spotted a five-year-old girl carrying a real china doll. Her arms ached to reach out and hold the doll, but the little girl poked her tongue out at Laura and turned away. Laura felt herself turning red. The storekeeper must have noticed, because he said, "Nellie Owens, that is no way to greet a stranger."

Laura remembered the name Nellie Owens and hoped that she would not run into the girl again.

Pa ordered four wagon wheels from Mr. Owens, the storekeeper, so that he could build another wagon for the family. The family would need a wagon to get supplies from town and for family outings. Laura was proud of the fact that her pa could make everything on the wagon except the wheels, which called for the skills of a wheelwright.

That evening, when the three of them got back to their sod house on the banks of Plum Creek, they had lots to tell Ma and Carrie. Ma was delighted to hear that Walnut Grove was growing and that a schoolhouse was planned for the southern end of the town.

Within a week of moving into their new house, the family found life settling into a pattern. Each morning, soon after sunup, Pa went off to work on Mr. Nelson's farm. He hoped to earn enough money to buy a cow for the family and put in a crop of wheat. Meanwhile Ma stayed busy in the sod house, constantly sweeping the place out and making meals for everyone. This left Laura or Mary in charge of Carrie for long stretches at a time. Laura would take her little sister down to the creek, where newly budding willow trees draped in the water. She liked to imagine that they were curtains leading into another world.

At dinnertime it was Laura's job to bring a bucket of water up from the creek and wash the dishes when the meal was over. This was her favorite time of day. After the dishes were washed, the family would gather around the open door of the sod house. Pa would play his fiddle as they all looked out over the silvery surface of Plum Creek as the last rays of sun set over the endless prairie beyond.

For Laura, Sunday was the best day of all. On Sunday the whole family would walk into town to attend church. The minister was a kindly man named the Reverend Mr. Alden. He was a home missionary for the Congregational Church, bringing Christianity to a number of pioneer towns in the newly opened West. This meant that he was not present at every Sunday service, because he was responsible for several other churches from Waseca to Marshall. Laura liked it most when Mr. Alden was in town and leading the service.

Because there was no church building in town, the families who made up the congregation met in the home of Mr. and Mrs. Kennedy. Laura would not have admitted it to her family, but she loved being with the Kennedy family more than she loved Sunday school. The Kennedys had five children, and their youngest, Nettie, was the same age as Laura. Nettie and Laura were soon best friends, and sometimes Laura was even allowed to stay at the Kennedy home for the afternoon and play with Nettie.

Ma and Pa were the first people to be baptized in the new congregation, and after their baptism, they promised to be strong supporters of the church. In August the church families decided it was time to erect a church building. A site for the church was purchased right next to where the schoolhouse was going to be built.

It was exciting for Laura to watch the church building go up. Her father helped out with the carpentry work whenever he could, though all of the men had to take time off in September to harvest their wheat crops.

The Ingallses' wheat crop was not particularly large because Mr. Hanson had not plowed many acres before he left to go west. Still, Pa told the girls, they would have enough wheat to make flour and feed the oxen through the winter. Next year, he said smiling, they would have a much bigger crop, and they would have a new house and horses too.

There was a push to finish the new Congregational church building before winter set in, and soon all that remained to do was to order a bell for the belfry. Pa had been planning to buy himself a new pair of boots for the winter, but he decided to donate the money toward buying a bell. The bell arrived in Walnut Grove by train a week after it was ordered. It was packed inside a thick wooden crate, and it took many men from the community to hoist it up into place in the belfry.

With the new church building finished, it was time to hold a dedication service. On December 20, 1874, Charles Ingalls hitched his two new horses to the wagon he had built, and everyone climbed aboard for the ride into Walnut Grove. When they arrived at the new Union Congregational Church, they found the place brimming with people. They made their way inside and found a place to sit in one of the pews just as the dedication service began. The congregation stood and sang a hymn, and then Mr. Alden prayed. Then the people sang another hymn, after which the Reverend Mr. Cobb, a member of the Congregational Home Missionary Society, preached a sermon. When the sermon was over, Mr. Alden stood and offered a prayer of dedication for the new church building.

Laura hardly heard a word that was uttered during the service. Her attention was focused on the Christmas tree at the front of the church. She thought it was the most beautiful Christmas tree she had ever seen. The tree was decorated with streamers made from lengths of brightly colored paper. But what had really caught Laura's attention were all the presents that hung from the branches of the tree. Laura hoped that at least one of them was for her.

When Mr. Alden finished his prayer, he turned his attention to the Christmas tree. He explained that the presents on the tree had been collected and sent by the members of his congregation in Waseca. Mrs. Tower, one of the women in the church, helped distribute the gifts to the children. Laura could feel her heart pounding as Mrs. Tower walked down the aisle toward her and handed her a present. She could hardly believe what it was—a little brown fur cape and shawl, which she immediately fell in love with. Ma smiled at her and patted her on the leg as a way of congratulating her for receiving such a nice gift.

More gifts were handed out. By the time the evening was over, Laura had also received a pair of red mittens, a bag filled with candy and popcorn, and a gleaming white china jewel box with a miniature teapot and cup and saucer painted in gold on top.

As she rode back home in the wagon, Laura could not imagine a better Christmas party than the one she had just been to. The fur cape was wrapped around her, and the other gifts sat at her side. As the wagon rumbled along over the prairie, Laura hoped that she would be at the church for the Christmas party next year and the year after that. Laura had no way of knowing that the following year would be the most trying year her family had ever endured.

Chapter 8

The Strange Cloud

The winter snow did not come until after the new year in 1875, but soon the land was covered with snow as deep as any the Ingalls family had experienced in the past. The sod dugout kept them warm and cozy, though it was a struggle to get the door open each morning. Pa would push his shoulder against it as hard as he could, and when it budged a little, he would reach his hand around and start scooping the snow away from it until it opened.

At first Laura was intrigued by the snow, which clung to the plum trees along the edge of Plum Creek. The creek itself froze over. For most of the day Laura stayed inside, mending clothes, making a red-and-white patchwork quilt, and keeping Carrie occupied. This was no easy task, and on special occasions Ma would let them get out her button box and string buttons. Ma owned a single novel, titled *Millbank*, which she read to Pa and the girls so many times during the winter that Laura eventually knew portions of it by heart.

Finally, much to Laura's delight, the spring thaw arrived. As the snow slowly melted, it turned Plum Creek into a foaming swirl of brown water. The creek had so much water in it that it burst its banks, and the water came right up to the door of the dugout. But the dugout was perched just high enough on the creek bank that no water actually came inside. Laura loved to watch the surging creek, though her parents warned her not to go near it while it was in flood stage.

Laura continued to watch the creek, and slowly the water flowing down it began to recede, so much so that one particular day Laura came outside and noticed that the plank bridge that Pa had built across the creek was visible again. The water was just lapping against the bottom of the bridge. As she stood and watched, Laura somehow felt the bridge and the creek calling to her to come and play. Finally she gave in to the beckoning. She took off her shoes and stockings and left them by the door and descended down the muddy steps that led to the bridge.

Laura walked out onto the bridge and sat down right in the middle of it. She lowered her legs over the edge of the bridge into the water and felt the water surge around them. The water was cold from the melting snow and felt strangely refreshing, so refreshing, in fact, that she rolled over on her belly and lowered her arms into the water as well. The water swirled across her arms and splashed up onto the bridge, wetting her dress. Laura wiggled forward to get more of her body into the water. Suddenly she was aware of the water tugging on her harder than ever. The water tugged so hard that it began to pull her from the bridge. In a panic Laura realized that she was too far into the water, and her efforts to get back onto the bridge only served to flip her right off of it and completely into the water.

Instinctively Laura reached up her arms and managed to grab the edge of the plank bridge before the water swept her downstream. She pulled hard with her arms until she managed to hook her chin over the edge of the bridge as well. She tried to yell for help, but the sound of the roaring water blocked her cry. The water was so cold that Laura felt her fingers and toes go numb. She was scared, very scared. She did not want to be swept away and drown. She had to do something. Slowly she edged first one arm and then the other across the plank and gripped its far edge. This gave her better leverage, and she pulled with all her might. Slowly she felt her chest rising up the edge of the plank. She kicked with her feet and pulled even harder with her arms. Moments later her body slipped up onto the top of the plank. She was safe!

Laura lay still for a few moments, gasping deeply for breath. Her heart was still thumping wildly as she crawled on hands and knees off the plank. The muddy creek bank never felt so good under her feet. She scrabbled back up to the door of the sod house, picked up her shoes and stockings, and stepped inside.

"Where have you been," Ma asked, looking up from her sewing. "Oh, my goodness. What happened? Quick, let's get you out of those wet clothes."

Laura unbuttoned her dress and peeled it off, and then Ma wrapped a towel around her and led her over to stand by the fire.

"Did you fall into the creek?" Ma asked as she dried Laura off.

"Not exactly. I kind of went in," Laura replied.

Ma went on drying Laura and listened quietly as Laura explained what had happened. When she had dried her off, Ma said, "You have been very naughty, Laura. You know we told you not to go near the creek until the thaw is over, but you disobeyed. But how can I punish you? You nearly drowned, and I am just glad you are alive."

After the incident on the bridge, Laura tried harder than ever to do what she was told, though it was a struggle at times.

Finally the thaw ended, and it was time for Pa to start plowing. He hitched up the two horses, and from sunup to sundown he plowed acre after acre of virgin prairie. He worked so hard that at night he was too tired even to play his fiddle, but he was filled with hope that this year he was going to have a wonderful crop of wheat.

One day, after he had plowed his land and planted his wheat crop, Pa went into town alone. He returned home late in the afternoon with a wagonload of machine-hewn lumber and store-bought nails. Everyone in the house was surprised, but Pa explained that the lumberyard owner had allowed him to buy the wood on credit because he had planted such a large crop of wheat. The crop seemed certain to fetch a high price once it was shipped back east to market by train.

Laura skipped for joy when she realized that they were going to have a new house before summer. As if that were not enough for her to take in, Pa also announced that work on building the schoolhouse in town was proceeding fast and he had enrolled Laura and Mary in the school.

It was hard for Laura to believe so many changes were happening at once. The next morning she and Mary got up extra early to watch their father start work on the house. Pa explained that the first thing he had to do was dig the foundation. The site he had chosen for the house was on a rise on the other side of the creek.

Two weeks after Pa began work on the new house, word came that the new school was ready to open. There was a flurry of activity as Ma put the finishing touches on the girls' new calico dresses and finished knitting stockings for them. Laura was eight years old by now, and although she was small for her age, she felt every inch grown up when she and Mary started out across the prairie for school the first morning. They walked straight and tall, each silently trying to imagine what the day would bring.

When they arrived at school, both girls were greeted by friends they had made at church and other social events. Laura got to share a desk with her friend Nettie, though having Nellie Owens sitting directly in front of them marred the experience. Nellie was pretty, smart, and rich, and she wrinkled up her nose at having to sit near a "country girl." Laura found it hard to resist reaching over and pulling Nellie's long, blonde braids, and in no time at all the two girls had become sworn enemies.

Nevertheless Laura loved attending school and was proud of the progress she made in reading and spelling. Each afternoon she and Mary walked home across the prairie, stopping to survey Pa's wheat crop on the way. At first the wheat looked like a layer of green fuzz on the dark earth. Then the plants grew bigger and turned into a blanket of green. Pa inspected the crop each day before he went to work on the house.

The girls had been attending school for two months when one day Pa called them aside on their way home. "The house is complete," he proudly told them.

Laura looked the place over. It was beautiful. The walls were made of pine planks neatly overlapped, and the floor was made of tongue-and-groove pine that fit tightly together and made a wonderful, smooth floor. The roof was made of store-bought shingles that were thin and even. Laura had to admit that the place looked better than most of the houses in Walnut Grove, especially since it had glass windows and machine-hewn doors with white china doorknobs. Inside, the house was divided into two large rooms, and a ladder led up the wall to an attic that ran the length of the house. The attic also had tongue-and-groove pine floors and glass windows at either end. This was going to be Laura and Mary's bedroom.

"Can you girls keep a secret?" Pa asked as he beckoned them to the back room of the house.

Mary and Laura nodded together.

"Then look what I have for your ma. I secretly brought it in from town and installed it. It's a surprise, and I think she's going to like it," Pa said.

"It's beautiful, Pa," Laura said while Mary ran her hand over the black, cast-iron cookstove that sat in the corner by the back door. A stovepipe ran up through the attic floor and on out through the roof.

"Now you girls promise you won't tell Ma? I want to see the look on her face tomorrow when we move in."

"We promise," Laura said for her and for Mary, though she knew it was going to be hard not to tell Ma the wonderful news. And it was not easy for Laura not to blurt out the secret she was keeping that night as Ma began to pack up the family belongings for the move. But somehow she managed to keep silent, though she had to bite her tongue several times.

The next morning Pa pulled the wagon up to the top of the creek bank, and the family loaded their belongings into it. When the wagon was full, Pa drove it down the bank, forded Plum Creek, and headed for the new house on the rise. While he did that, Ma, Mary, Laura, and Carrie, each carrying an armful of belongings, walked over the plank bridge and made their way to the new house. Pa already had the wagon pulled up in front of the place and stood waiting by the front door.

Ma carried her armful of belongings into the house, and Pa followed her inside. Laura, Mary, and Carrie ran to catch up so that they could see their mother's surprise at seeing the new cook-stove. They arrived just in time to hear Ma gasp, "My land, Charles, what's that?"

"It's your new cookstove," Pa said proudly. "I wanted to surprise you."

"Surprise me! You've certainly done that! But, Charles, you shouldn't have," Ma exclaimed.

Pa grinned from ear to ear, and Laura and Mary danced in circles with delight at Ma's surprise and at the fact that they had kept the secret.

Once their belongings had been carried into the new house, Ma started a fire in the cookstove, and before long she had corn cakes cooking on top of it.

Over the next several days, Laura, Mary, and Carrie helped their mother make curtains and hang them in the windows of the new house while Pa put up shelves in the kitchen for Ma to put the cooking utensils and supplies on.

Laura loved living in the new house. Most of all she liked her new bedroom in the attic. From the attic window she could see out across Pa's field of wheat, which was beginning to turn gold. As she looked out over the vast field, she imagined the lux-ury the Ingalls family would be enjoying a year from now as a result of all the money Pa was going to make from his bountiful harvest.

At lunch one hot afternoon in late summer, Pa announced that the wheat would be ready for harvest in a week. "That field will yield at least forty bushels an acre, and right now wheat is selling for a dollar a bushel. When it comes to money, things are finally starting to look up," Pa said.

As Pa spoke, Laura noticed out the window that it was getting strangely dark. Ma also noticed and said, "I believe a storm is coming."

Pa got up from the table and went outside to see. With his wheat so close to harvest, the last thing he needed was for it to be damaged by a storm.

"Caroline," Laura heard Pa call moments later.

Ma got up and walked out the door, followed by Mary, Laura, and Carrie.

"What do you make of that?" Pa asked Ma.

Ma stared at the black cloud blotting out the sun, as did Laura and Mary. The cloud was unlike anything Laura had ever seen before. In fact, upon closer look, it did not seem like a cloud at all but more like black snowflakes fluttering in the air. But it couldn't be snowflakes. This was summer on the prairie, and the weather was clear and hot and steamy. There was also no wind, and the cloud was moving over the prairie faster than the wind could have pushed it. As the cloud got closer, it made a strange noise, like hail pelting against the ground.

Pa was standing scratching his head when suddenly the sky began to rain bugs—big, green grasshoppers, to be precise, their flimsy wings beating so fast that they were almost impossible to see. The grasshoppers clung to everyone's hair and clothes, and their bulging eyes peered at everyone. Laura tried to brush the insects off, but they kept on coming. Mary ran inside in fright. Ma and Laura followed her, and once inside they quickly closed the windows and doors to keep the bugs out. Soon Pa came inside. He stood by the window and watched as the grasshoppers kept coming. The insects beat on the roof and against the side of the house like hail.

For days the barrage of grasshoppers kept coming, keeping Laura inside the hot, stuffy house. After many days Laura noticed out the window that there seemed to be fewer grasshoppers, until finally no more grasshoppers were descending on the land. Even so, it was hard for Laura, or anyone else for that matter, to fathom the destruction the grasshoppers had left behind. Not a blade of wheat or prairie grass was left standing upright for miles around. The plum trees that lined the banks of Plum Creek had been stripped bare of the leaves and fruit, as had the willow trees. And the dead bodies of the insects were inches thick in some places. So many grasshoppers had died on the railroad tracks that the trains had difficulty gaining enough traction on the slippery tracks to move forward.

Pa stared blankly at what had once been his bumper crop of wheat, and Laura knew that he was thinking about the house, which he had bought on credit against the promise of a good wheat crop. Now nothing was left, not even enough grains of wheat to provide the family with flour to see them through the long winter months.

Then one morning, not too long after the grasshoppers had ravaged the land, Laura awoke to find

Pa gone. "He's gone to find work," Ma explained in a controlled voice. "Uncle Peter wrote to say that the grasshoppers didn't make it as far east as the Zumbro River and that there was plenty of work around the area there for able men." Laura could sense from her mother's voice that now was a time to be strong, so she did not cry at the thought of her father leaving.

When Laura returned to school, she learned that many of the men and boys throughout the area had headed east in search of work. It made her feel better to know that Pa was with people he knew—men who would remind him of home.

Mr. Nelson, their neighbor, helped out around the farm where he could, chopping wood and bringing letters from Pa when they arrived at the post office in Walnut Grove. For the most part, however, it was Laura, Mary, and Ma who kept the family together during the fall of 1875. Each Saturday they waited anxiously to see if there was a letter from Pa, and the letters came like clockwork. Sometimes the envelope contained money along with the letter, while at other times Pa would simply explain how he was working hard and earning every cent he could.

Then at last, on a crisp fall day, Pa came home. He walked into the house and hoisted Carrie into the air. Laura giggled with delight and waited for her turn to be lifted up.

Soon the family were seated around the table. Pa had bought some coffee in town, and soon the coffeepot was simmering on the stove as he told of how he had worked the crops in eastern Minnesota and now he had a purseful of money. He had made a dollar a day while he was away.

Laura had expected things to return to normal once her father had returned, but they did not. She and Mary soon learned that Ma had been keeping a secret the whole time Pa was away. Another baby was on the way and was due to be born sometime in November. Pa wanted Ma to be closer to help when the time came for the baby's birth, so he announced that the family would be moving into Walnut Grove for the winter. He even had a job as a carpenter lined up there for the next five months.

Everything happened so fast. Before Laura knew it, the family was packed up and moving into a small house just down the road from the schoolhouse. This meant that Laura and Mary could go to school all winter long and did not have to worry about getting trapped in a blizzard. The family went back to regularly attending church and Sunday school, something they had not done while Pa was away. Each Sunday morning Laura loved hearing the sound of "Pa's church bell," as she called it, and joining the procession of neighbors dressed in their Sunday bonnets or black suits on their way to church.

Before long, Laura's mother gave birth to a fourth child, a son, whom they named Charles Fredrick Ingalls. The girls soon shortened the name to Freddie.

With the arrival of a baby brother, Laura had more chores than ever to do around the house, not to mention taking turns looking after Freddie. Still, despite the added work, she was glad to have a baby brother and hoped that he would grow up to be just like her father.

As soon as the spring thaw began, Pa moved the family back to the house at Plum Creek. Although it was much more convenient to live in town, he missed the wide-open spaces, as did Laura, who breathed in the wonderful prairie air as they unpacked their belongings once again.

Both girls were still able to attend school, and each day they walked past Pa's newly plowed and planted wheat field. This time, though, no one in the area was overly excited when the wheat sprouts broke through the ground. Each person knew the destructive potential of the grasshopper eggs that lay in the ground. And sure enough, within days of the wheat peeking through the ground, the grass-hoppers hatched and ate every single sprout. Laura watched brokenhearted as her father walked along the rows of his destroyed wheat crop.

Everyone in Walnut Grove was in the same situation. People were in dire straits financially, and a pall fell over the place. One by one the businesses in town began to close. Pa walked into town most days looking for work, but so did just about every other man in the area. A plague of grasshoppers had turned Pa's dream of owning a farm in Minnesota into a nightmare. Each night Laura heard Ma and Pa sit on the doorstep and talk quietly about how the family would survive the next winter. Their voices were low and discouraged.

Chapter 9

Burr Oak

Two weeks later Laura found herself sitting in a new covered wagon, one that Pa had bought with the money he made from selling the house and property at Plum Creek. The Ingalls family were on the move again, but this time they were headed east, not west. Pa had come up with a plan: the family would spend the summer at Uncle Peter's farm, where Pa could find work, and then they would head south to Burr Oak, Iowa, to help run a hotel. Mr. Steadman, the new owner of the hotel, had lived in Walnut Grove before moving to Burr Oak, and he had offered Pa a job helping out at the hotel.

For the first time ever, the members of the Ingalls family felt no joy or anticipation about moving. Throughout the journey baby Freddie cried constantly, and Ma and Pa hardly spoke. Laura tried hard not to think of the friends and the house she had left behind because when she did, tears slid down her cheeks.

One hundred sixty miles later, the wagon rolled to a halt in front of Uncle Peter and Aunt Eliza's house in Wabasha County. The families had not seen each other for two years, and Laura was excited to see her cousins again, particularly Peter.

As it turned out, all the children had a lot of fun that summer. Since having two families living together in a single house did not seem to double the chores that needed to be done, the children had lots of spare time to run in the sun and bathe in the river. And while the children played, Pa went off to work in the fields around Wabasha County. He made good money, especially during harvest time. When the harvest was over, it was time for the family to reload their wagon and head for Iowa.

Just as they were about to set out, Freddie got sick. The doctor wasn't exactly sure what the child was suffering from, and none of the remedies he suggested seemed to help Freddie get better. Meanwhile, Pa paced in the doorway, Ma sobbed into a handkerchief, and the three Ingalls sisters tried to stay out of their parents' way. Then on Sunday, August 27, 1876, the thing that Ma and Pa feared happened. Freddie died at nine months of age and was buried the following day on the outskirts of South Troy, just south of the Zumbro River.

Freddie's funeral was a solemn affair, and soon after it was over, the Ingalls family left the area. The cold, gray weather mimicked their mood as the

wagon rolled south. Hours would pass without anyone saying a word, and Pa's fiddle never left its case
throughout the whole journey.

Burr Oak was located in northeastern Iowa, just
south of the border with Minnesota, and was surrounded by rolling limestone hills and forests of oak
trees. Twenty years earlier the place had been a
major crossroads for wagon trains heading west. At
one time up to three hundred wagons a day were
passing through town, but by 1876, when Laura and
her family arrived, Burr Oak was a sleepy little town.

Pa drove the wagon through the main street of
town and stopped at one of the two local hotels. The
place was called Burr Oak House, and it was a large,
white, wood-frame building with a veranda that
faced the street and ran the length of the hotel. At
first Laura thought the place was two stories high,
but when she ran around back, she discovered that
it was actually three stories. The hotel sat on a
bank that sloped steeply away from the road, hid-
ing the third story from those who saw the building
at street level.

The inside of the hotel seemed larger to Laura
than it did from the outside. Downstairs had a barroom, kitchen, dining room, and parlor, and upstairs
were the guest bedrooms. The Ingalls family moved
into one of the upstairs rooms. It was a strange situation for Laura to be sharing her home with a
revolving cast of strangers. Some of the people were
nice and polite, but others got drunk, and one even
shot off his gun inside, blasting a hole through the
dining room door.

Ma tried to keep the children upstairs as much as possible. During the day the three girls were sent off to attend school located on a hill along Spring Street. Pa spent much of his day making repairs to the hotel, and in the evenings he would sit in the parlor and play his fiddle while Ma cleaned up after the guests and helped prepare meals in the kitchen. In the evenings Laura and Mary were expected to help serve the meals to the guests, but Ma always kept a watchful eye on them. There are good strangers and bad strangers, she constantly reminded the girls.

Laura longed for the carefree life she had led on the prairie when Pa would come in at night holding a rabbit he had caught and Ma would laugh with delight. When Christmas rolled around, she wished she were part of the congregation back in Walnut Grove, though when she thought about it honestly, she doubted that many of the people she knew had been able to stay on in the town after the invasion of grasshoppers.

In January Mr. Steadman admitted to Pa that the hotel was not profitable and that he intended to sell it if he got a good offer for the place. Once again the Ingalls family did not have a stable place to live. Then, much to Ma's relief, they moved out of the hotel into rooms above the grocery store next door. Pa began working at a local sawmill and did odd jobs while Ma looked after the rooms and the children. On February 7, 1877, not long after they had moved into the rooms above the grocery store, Laura celebrated a gloomy tenth birthday.

When school started up again, Laura was advanced to the next class, a fact that made her very

proud. Her new teacher, Mr. Reed, put great importance on reading aloud, and although he had fifty-
seven pupils in his class, he took time to encourage
Laura to read and recite as best she could.

During this time Laura cherished her *Independent Fifth Reader*, and especially the poems "Polish
Boy," "Paul Revere," and "Old Tubal Cain," which
were in the book. Each night Laura practiced reading the poems the way Mr. Reed had shown her
until she knew them by heart.

In February Ma told Laura and Mary that she was
expecting another baby sometime in May. Laura
was excited about the prospect until she recalled
the pain of losing Freddie, and then her excitement
turned to anxiety. The question of whether they
should continue to live above the store, since there
were so many steps for Ma to climb, was also raised.
The matter was swiftly decided one day when something happened at Burr Oak House next door.

"Hairpin" Jim, a man Pa had gotten to know
quite well, sat for several days drinking in the bar.
Eventually he became so drunk and so exhausted
that he fell to the floor, where people walked
around him and left him unconscious. By the time
Hairpin Jim finally regained consciousness, everyone had left the barroom. Jim crawled back up onto
his feet and reached for a cigar. When he struck a
match to light the cigar, the fumes of alcohol were
so thick around his mouth that they ignited. Flames
raced down Jim's throat, and Hairpin Jim died in
an instant.

Laura was both repulsed and fascinated when
she heard of the gruesome event, but for Pa it was

the motivation he needed. He announced, "I won't have my wife and daughters living next to that confounded hotel one day longer!"

True to his word, he found a small, redbrick house at the other end of town for the family to stay in. Everyone liked living in the house much better than living in the rooms above the grocery store. The house was located on the edge of town, and Laura was able to go for long walks in the oak woods nearby. But best of all, Pa bought the family a cow, and Ma resumed making her wonderful buttermilk, butter, and cheese as she had done back in Minnesota.

With a new baby on the way, Ma needed Laura to help around the house, so Laura took several months off school. Then on May 23, 1877, while Laura was out on a long errand, the baby was born. She was a golden-haired, blue-eyed girl whom Ma and Pa named Grace.

Grace Ingalls was a healthy, strong child right from the start, and Laura soon stopped worrying about her dying as Freddie had. Instead, she enjoyed a wonderful summer of playing with friends, watching the cow graze in the nearby woods, and helping take care of Grace.

On Friday and Saturday nights, Mr. Reed, Laura's schoolteacher, arranged entertainment nights filled with music, plays, and recitations. Sundays were spent attending church and going on Sunday school picnics, complete with lemonade and homemade cakes. Everything seemed perfect, and Laura hoped she would spend many summers at Burr Oak.

One fall day Laura arrived home from school to find Mrs. Starr talking to her mother. Mrs. Starr was the wife of the local doctor and belonged to one of the richest families in Burr Oak. Laura had always liked Dr. and Mrs. Starr—until she heard what the woman was saying.

"You have to think of the girl," Mrs. Starr said, putting her arm around Laura. "Now that my own two daughters have grown up and moved away, I have room to take in another one and raise her as my own. It's very lonely in such a big house, and a lively little girl like Laura could help me with the work and keep me company."

Laura stood completely still. "A lively little girl like Laura!" Could Mrs. Starr possibly mean she wanted to take Laura to live with her? The next sentence left no doubt.

"I know it would be a sacrifice for you, Mrs. Ingalls," Mrs. Starr went on, "but would you please consider letting me adopt Laura?"

Adopt? Had she heard right? Laura looked at her mother, desperate to see her reaction. But the look on Ma's face was hard for her to interpret. After a long pause, Laura felt her stomach lurch as she waited for Ma to say something—anything.

Finally Ma spoke up. "Thank you for the offer, Mrs. Starr. You are right. Laura is a lively little girl, and great company. I couldn't possibly get along without her myself."

Laura wanted to run over to her mother and hug her as hard as she could, but she stayed where she was, smiling.

That night, as she lay in bed beside Mary, Laura thought hard about her family's situation. She had enjoyed a wonderful, carefree summer, but had the rest of the family? She began to think about her father working long hours in the sawmill and how little money he was paid for his labor. She wondered about Ma, who sold some of the butter she churned and made pies to sell from the wild blackberries the three older girls collected. Perhaps, Laura decided, her family was not doing as well as they had all hoped. Why else would someone even imagine that Ma would let her be adopted?

Laura's suspicion about the family's predicament was confirmed when she overheard a conversation between Pa and Ma. It was about the overdue rent on the house and the outstanding doctor's bill for Grace's birth. Pa sounded defeated and said that he had little hope of finding a steady job during the winter.

Laura was not too surprised when early one morning Ma woke her and the others and they started loading up the wagon again. Ma explained that they had sold the cow to pay their debts and that Pa thought it was time to leave Burr Oak. Laura hated to think they were leaving such a nice place. The only thing that comforted her was the fact that they were headed northwest, back to Walnut Grove, Minnesota.

As the wagon rattled along, Laura thought about the time they had been away from Walnut Grove. It had been only a year, but it seemed much longer. Laura was ten years old now, and she felt much

more grown up—and a little weary. In the past
twelve months, she had lost a brother, she had lived
in a hotel and several other places, and Ma had
been asked to adopt her out.

The trip back to Minnesota was fast and pre-
dictable, and in record time the Ingallses' wagon
pulled up outside the Ensigns' house in Walnut
Grove. Mr. and Mrs. Ensign were old church friends
of Ma and Pa's, and they welcomed the family back
with open arms. Everyone slept in the house that
night, and the following morning Mr. and Mrs.
Ensign invited the Ingalls family to stay with them
through the winter. This could save on the costs of
groceries, and Pa could chop wood and hunt for
both families.

Pa and Ma happily agreed to the arrangement,
and Laura was thrilled with their decision. The
three-room house was very crowded with eleven
people living in it, but all of the children got along
well. Anna Ensign was thirteen years old, just a little older than Mary. Willard was fourteen, and
Howard was ten, like Laura.

While Pa hunted for work the following morning,
the Ingalls and Ensign children went off to explore
the town. The town had changed very little in the
year Laura had been away. Some families had left
because of the grasshopper invasion, but a surpris-
ing number had stayed and somehow made it
through. Thankfully the Kennedys were still there,
and Laura had a joyous reunion with Nettie. The
Congregational church now had a manse and a permanent minister, the Reverend Mr. Moses. Walnut

Grove now had a hotel as well, owned by William Masters, who happened to be the man who had owned Burr Oak House before the Steadmans had bought it from him. Laura realized that although the West seemed endless, often the same people criss-crossed it again and again, looking for a chance to make a solid living.

Life fell into a pleasant pattern in Walnut Grove as the three oldest Ingalls children, along with the three Ensign children, attended school and Sunday school. Laura was promoted to the same grammar book Mary was on, and she excelled in spelling. Laura was very proud of her spelling abilities, especially since the town held regular Friday-night spelling bees.

Everyone, both parents and children, would congregate in the schoolhouse. Lamps hissed around the room, lighting it, and when it was time to start the competition, the teacher would ring a bell. At the sound of the bell, the parents would gather at the back of the room and stand quietly while the children took a seat at their desks. The teacher would call the two best spellers in the school to the front, and then the students would take turns picking the other students for their side until all were chosen. Each side would then line up along the walls, facing each other, and the spelling bee would begin.

The teacher would say a word clearly, and then the first student would repeat the word and spell it. If a child spelled the word incorrectly, he or she was disqualified and had to sit back down at his or her desk. On and on this process would go until one person was left standing, and that person was declared the winner of the spelling bee.

Laura was glad that she could spell so well, because it meant that she was always one of the last children to have to sit down, and on more than one occasion, she was declared the winner.

Pa found work at the new hotel, and soon he was able to save enough money to buy lumber so that in spring he could build the family a new house, located on the outskirts of town. Of course Laura knew Pa would sooner have bought another farm, but she knew he did not have enough money to do that. As soon as he had finished building the new house, Pa rented a storefront on the main street of town and set up a butchery. He did a roaring business, cutting up livestock and wild game.

Laura was also put to work. With school out for the summer, Mrs. Masters asked Pa and Ma if Laura could work for her at the hotel. She promised to pay Laura fifty cents a week. Ma and Pa talked about it and decided that it would be good for Laura, so she took the job.

On Laura's first day, Mrs. Masters explained that she wanted Laura to help with washing dishes, serving the guests their meals, assisting in the kitchen, and looking after her baby daughter during quiet times. Laura especially liked looking after the baby, because the baby slept most of the time, allowing Laura to read copies of the *New York Ledger*. Laura particularly enjoyed reading the stories in the magazine. Somehow they carried her away to a life and places beyond the prairie.

As she chopped vegetables and stirred the iron pot on the stove in the kitchen, Laura often found herself wondering what she would do when summer was over. Would she get to go back to school? She hoped so. She hated to think that she might spend the rest of her life cooking and scrubbing for a living.

Chapter 10

Working on the Railroad

A contest, with a prize! Laura could hardly believe her luck. One Bible verse was going to be announced each Sunday afternoon at the new Methodist Sunday school, and the child who could recite and remember the most verses in the correct order would win the contest. Laura was sure she was going to be the winner, and she started attending the Methodist Sunday school each week.

As fall approached, Laura's time helping Mrs. Masters at the hotel came to an end, and Ma and Pa sent Laura out to stay at the Hurley farm, where Laura cared for Mrs. Hurley, who was sick with an unknown illness. Laura was glad to be able to help both her family and the Hurley family, though she did get lonely and looked forward to Sundays, when she would walk into town and attend Sunday school and see her family. Her sister Mary was not well, and each Sunday Laura could see the worry lines etched deeper around Ma's eyes. Thankfully, baby Grace was thriving.

At the start of winter, Laura returned to Walnut Grove to live with her family. This was the time she was supposed to go back to school, but it turned out to be a winter filled with blizzards that blew in from the Arctic, and the school was often closed. One night in January Laura learned that five children were missing from a farm located along Plum Creek. The parents had driven into town for supplies, leaving their children at home. A storm had blown up, and the parents had been unable to get back to the farm until the next day. When they finally returned, they discovered that their children were gone. Pa guessed that the children had most likely tried to reach the barn together and lost their way in the blizzard.

The men of Walnut Grove banded together to search for the missing children. Laura wished she could help. She knew the three oldest children. One of the girls was in her class at school, and it was agonizing waiting for news of what had happened to the children. Finally Pa came riding back into town with the news that the children had been found in a snowdrift. Sadly, three of them, two boys and a girl, had frozen to death, while Laura's classmate and the baby brother she was holding were still alive. The heat from the girl's body had kept the baby alive. But one of the girl's legs had been badly frostbitten during the ordeal and would have to be amputated. It was a somber lesson for everyone in Walnut Grove. Winter could be deadly if you acted without thinking.

The funeral for the three dead children was held the day before Laura's twelfth birthday, casting a somber pall over her birthday celebration.

Despite the sadness and loss, life went on in Walnut Grove. In the spring Pa was elected as a trustee of the Congregational church, and then he was made a justice of the peace. This meant that he held trials in the family living room. Laura was fascinated by the tales she heard from listening behind the kitchen door.

In the spring of 1879, Mr. Masters built his own butcher shop next to the hotel, and Pa lost most of the business at his butchery to this new store. To make ends meet, he began doing various carpentry jobs, and Laura got a new job helping Mrs. Masters, who was suffering from fainting spells.

It was not a hopeful time for the Ingalls family, but things got a hundred times worse when one day Mary, who had not been completely well for months, started screaming from pain and ran a high fever. Ma sent for Dr. Hoyt, the local doctor, who told her to keep Mary as cool as possible. Mary was so ill that Ma did not hesitate to take her sewing scissors and cut off her daughter's beautiful golden hair. She told Laura that she hoped this would help to cool Mary down.

Laura was alarmed at how ill Mary was, and she was afraid that her sister might die. The adults around Mary seemed to think she would. Dr. Hoyt visited the house two or three times a day, and each time he shook his head. All day and all night either Ma or Pa was beside Mary's bed, and Laura's job was to keep Carrie and Grace as quiet as possible. On the fifth morning of Mary's illness, Laura awoke to find Dr. Hoyt at the house extra early.

"Mary's had a stroke," Ma told her gently, "and her face looks different now."

Laura braced herself and went over to see Mary. Mary looked terrible. Half of her face looked like it had sunk. Mary tried to speak, but only one side of her lips moved, and one eye blinked. However, the stroke marked a turning point, and Mary's temperature returned to normal. Then, just as she was getting her strength and facial movements and speech back, the unthinkable happened—Mary started to go blind. Dr. Hoyt called in another doctor, a man from New England who was the general surgeon for the railroad, but there was nothing either of them could do. Within two weeks Mary was totally blind.

The entire family was stunned. No one had ever heard of this happening to a fourteen-year-old girl. Laura wept at the thought of her sister never seeing anything again—not the open prairie, the way the wind bent the grass, or the way the prairie and the sky seemed to merge at the horizon. The days seemed longer now for Laura, who had to do Mary's chores as well as her own. Laura still found time to worry about what would happen to her sister.

The Ingalls family seemed to have little hope that their situation would improve, when unexpectedly

Aunt Docia arrived from Wisconsin. She had driven herself to Walnut Grove in a buggy, and she had a proposition for Pa. Her husband, Hiram, was a contractor on the railroad that was pushing west. He and his crew were working at the very end of the line that was inching into Dakota territory. Aunt Docia explained that Uncle Hiram needed to hire someone to serve as storekeeper, bookkeeper, and timekeeper, and he was willing to pay fifty dollars a month for the right man. She had come to see if that man might be her brother Charles Ingalls.

Laura watched as Pa's face brightened at the idea of working at the end of a railroad that was pushing ever westward. But Ma looked tired and dejected at the thought. That night Laura overheard her parents discussing the idea of Pa leaving first to take up the job and then the rest of the family following later.

"But what about Mary?" she heard her Ma ask. "There won't be any way to help her out there."

"There's no way to help her here," Pa replied softly.

"I just don't know if I could do it, Charles," Ma said. "We have friends here, and the children have school. I'm so tired of starting over."

Laura's parents talked on for some time until they came to a compromise. Pa promised Ma that if she would move this time, he would settle wherever they ended up and never ask her to move again.

This idea took Laura's breath away because she knew what it cost Pa, with his rambling ways, to make the promise.

Ma agreed to the compromise, and the next day everyone helped Pa get ready to leave with Aunt Docia. Ma made hardtack, a biscuit made of flour and water, for the journey, and Laura washed and ironed Pa's clothes. While they were doing this, Pa visited Mr. Masters, who agreed to buy the house and lot when Ma was ready to leave. Back at the house, Pa put the canvas top on the wagon and hitched up the horses. By midafternoon he and Aunt Docia were gone, headed west to the end of the railroad line.

The plan was for Ma, Laura, Mary, Carrie, and little Grace to travel a month later by train to Tracy, Minnesota, where Pa would pick them up in the wagon and take them to the railway workers' camp. While she was excited about heading west, Laura was also sad to be leaving Walnut Grove behind. Her last triumph in the town was to win the scripture memorization contest at the Methodist Sunday school. For her effort she was awarded a small, black leather Bible, which she packed at the bottom of her bag for the journey west.

Finally the departure day in September 1879 arrived. Ma woke Laura and her three sisters early and had them dress in their best dresses. After they packed the last few items into two suitcases, they left the house for the last time and headed for the railway station. At the station Ma bought three tickets on the train to Tracy. Carrie and Grace were both young enough to travel free. Then they all sat in the waiting room until the train arrived. An hour later Laura heard a screeching, clanging noise in the distance, and then she saw billows of smoke. The train was arriving. Laura described everything she saw to Mary as the steam locomotive ground to a halt with a loud hiss in front of the station platform.

Ma picked up one of the suitcases and Grace, and she led Carrie from the waiting room to the train. Laura carried the other suitcase in one hand and led Mary with her other hand. They walked across the wooden planks of the station platform, past boxcars and flat freight wagons loaded with lumber, to the carriage at the end of the train. The conductor took the suitcases from Ma and Laura, carried them inside the carriage, and lifted them up onto the luggage rack. Ma boarded the train and took a seat in the carriage. Laura guided Mary up the two metal steps that led into the carriage and then down the aisle to the seat in front of Ma. She then sat down by the window, with Mary next to her.

Laura could hardly believe it: she was finally on a train. She looked around and took everything in. The seats were upholstered in red velvet, the wooden interior was varnished, and windows ran the length of the carriage. Other people were riding in the carriage with them. A man with graying hair and a large bald spot on the crown of his head sat in the seat in front. Across from Ma and the girls sat another man, reading a newspaper and paying no attention to what was happening on the station platform outside. Farther back in the carriage, two young men sat next to each other. They both wore hats, and they were studying a large map. Several women were in the carriage as well. One of them had bright yellow hair, and another wore a sunbonnet. Laura tried her best to be Mary's eyes, describing to her sister in as much detail as she could what she was seeing.

As Laura was explaining the view to Mary, her words were soon drowned out by the shrill of the train whistle. Then all of a sudden the carriage lurched forward and slowly began to move. Laura could hear the locomotive huffing and puffing as the train gathered speed and the railway station slipped from view. She pressed her nose to the window and took her last look at Walnut Grove. She could see the spire on the Congregational church and the front of Mr. Masters's hotel. Then the train passed the schoolhouse and then the lumberyard, until the town finally receded and disappeared from view. The train continued to gather speed until the wheels made a rhythmic clickity-clack sound on the rails beneath the carriage. Laura could hardly believe how fast they were going. She guessed it must be at least twenty miles an hour. She had never gone that fast before in her life. The family had been lucky to cover twenty miles in a day when they traveled in the wagon across the prairie.

Fields and homesteads flashed past the windows of the carriage, and Laura watched as the wire strung on the telegraph poles alongside the railroad tracks sagged into big arcs between the poles.

The trip lasted only a morning, less than half the time it must have taken Pa to cover the same distance in the wagon. Soon the train pulled to a halt in Tracy, and Ma and the girls clambered out of the carriage and onto the station platform. Tracy was the current terminus of the railroad, and Laura watched with rapt attention as the steam engine was unhooked from the rest of the train and moved forward onto a large turntable that turned it around. The locomotive then steamed down a spur line that connected back to the main line at the eastern end of the station. Once it was on the main line, the locomotive backed up and was hooked to the back of the train for the return trip east. Laura had never seen such an ingenious device as the turntable with which to turn the engine around.

The conductor carried the two suitcases to the nearby hotel for Ma while Laura led Mary along by the arm. At the hotel Ma booked a room for them to stay in until Pa arrived, and then they all ate lunch in the hotel dining room.

It was late in the afternoon and long shadows were beginning to stretch across the prairie when Pa finally arrived in Tracy with the wagon. Everyone was happy to see him, and Laura gave him a long, hard hug. Pa explained that the railway camp was located beside the Big Sioux River two days' travel away to the west in Dakota territory. At first light in the morning they would set out in the wagon for the camp.

After spending the night in the hotel, the Ingalls family were up bright and early the next morning, and after eating breakfast in the dining room, they climbed up onto the wagon and set off west. They followed the newly laid railroad tracks as they went.

They spent the night camped beside the tracks and set off again the following morning.

The sun had set and a silvery moon shined above when Laura finally saw a speck of light in the distance. The light grew bigger as Pa guided the wagon forward, and soon Laura could see that it was coming from the window of a long, low shanty.

"This is what's left of the camp," Pa said as they approached. "Aunt Docia should have dinner waiting for us."

Sure enough, no sooner had Pa pulled the wagon to a halt than Aunt Docia threw open the door and called, "Welcome. Come on in quick. I just laid supper on the table."

By now Laura was so tired that all she really wanted to do was lie down and sleep, but since she was also hungry, she climbed out of the wagon and headed inside for supper. Sitting by the fireplace inside the shanty were Uncle Hiram and Laura's cousins Lena and Eugene. Lena was three months older than Laura, and the last time the two had been together was at the sugaring-off dance at Grandma and Grandpa Ingalls's big house back in the woods of Wisconsin five years before.

Throughout supper Aunt Docia talked incessantly, but Laura hardly took in a word she said. She ate her food as fast as she could and was glad when it was time for her to go to bed. Laura and Lena slept in a tent outside because there was no room in the shanty. The moment Laura lay down on the blanket on the hard ground, she was sound asleep.

The following morning Laura and Lena got up bright and early and explored the camp. As Laura soon discovered, there wasn't much to see. The Ingalls family had arrived at the railroad camp at Big Sioux just as the camp was being dismantled. Over breakfast Pa explained that the contractors building the railroad west had expected to make it only as far as the Big Sioux River before winter set in and they would have to stop work until the spring. But they were ahead of schedule and had pushed on across the river and farther west. As a result, the camp was being dismantled and rebuilt thirty-five miles farther west at a place called Silver Lake. As the camp was being carried away, surveyors were busy laying out a new town that would be built on the site of the old camp. Like Walnut Grove, this new town would service the families that would move into the area to live and farm now that the railroad had opened up the area. Pa also explained that the family would be pushing west to the new camp at Silver Lake in a few days. In fact, he had already been out to the new campsite and had built a shanty for the family.

Sure enough, within days of arriving at Big Sioux, the Ingalls family climbed back onto the wagon and headed for the new campsite. Once across the river, they again followed the railroad. Soon the rails petered out, and they followed the prepared bed where the rails would go. Laura listened as Pa told Ma that it took a lot more time to grade, compact, and prepare the bed for the railway line than it did to lay the actual rails, not to mention building trestle bridges over the rivers, creeks, and ravines. In spring when the snow melted, a crew would come back and begin laying the rails from where they left off.

It was late in the evening when they finally arrived at the Silver Lake camp. Laura had fallen asleep in the back of the wagon, but she woke up with a start when the wagon came to a halt. What had startled her was not the wagon stopping but a familiar voice, that of her Uncle Henry. Pa had known he was at the camp all along but had kept it a surprise. Even better, Laura's cousins Charles and Louisa were with him. As with Lena and Eugene, Laura had not seen them since she left Wisconsin five years before. They had changed so much that Laura did not think she would have recognized them, especially Charles, who was practically a man now.

Ma was speechless as she climbed down off the wagon and embraced her brother. Laura watched as tears were soon running down Ma's cheeks at the happy reunion. Uncle Henry explained that he and the two children were earning money working on the railroad so that they could move farther west to the Big Horn country of Montana. Aunt Polly would be joining them there once they had a place to live. As Uncle Henry explained all this, Laura could see a faraway look in Pa's eyes, and she wondered whether he had forgotten the promise that he had made to Ma.

But Pa had not forgotten. However he may have felt about Uncle Henry's heading farther west, he explained the next morning that this was as far as the Ingalls family was going. When the railroad camp moved, they would be staying behind. As a flock of birds took flight off the lake and soared in the sky above the vast and open prairie, Pa pointed out the site he had chosen for their new, permanent home. "See that knoll over there," he said. "That's where I want our homestead to be."

Laura studied the low hill Pa was pointing to. "It'll make a fine homestead for us, Pa," she said.

"What does it look like?" Mary asked, tugging on Laura's sleeve.

A pang of guilt shot through Laura. In all the excitement she had forgotten to be Mary's eyes. She quickly described the scene to her sister as best she could. Then it was time to unload the wagon into the shanty Pa had built for the family.

While Ma arranged things inside the shanty to make it like home, Laura took Mary by the hand and led her around the Silver Lake camp, explaining what it was like as they went.

"There's a lake," she explained. "It's not very big, but it glistens like silver in the sun. The camp is on the northern shore of the lake. It's made up of a number of shanties—long, low wooden buildings like the one Pa built for us. Some of them have families living in them, and others are bunkrooms for the men to live in, and one serves as a dining room and kitchen where they eat. In the middle of all the shanties is a large, wood-frame house. Pa says this is the surveyor's house. And off to the west of the lake the men are building the new railroad. You can't actually see them, just the cloud of dust where they are working."

Slowly autumn settled over Silver Lake. The prairie grass turned a dull brown color, and each day flocks of geese and other birds flew overhead heading south. The mornings grew cooler and cooler, until most mornings frost lay on the ground. Still the work went on. The men kept pressing west with the railroad, far beyond the western edge of Silver Lake. In fact, they pushed so far west that another camp had to be established, and many of the men staying at the Silver Lake camp moved there.

During this time Laura was kept very busy helping Ma with the cooking and cleaning and taking care of the children. Her cousins, particularly Lena, who helped Aunt Docia cook for the men, were also kept busy with their various chores, and so Laura did not get to spend much time with them.

Then one day Aunt Docia, Uncle Hiram, Lena, and Eugene stopped by the shanty to say good-bye. They were headed west to the next railroad camp. Their departure was followed soon afterward by that of Uncle Henry, Charles, and Louisa. Slowly the men and families at the Silver Lake camp began to drift away. Most were headed home for the winter and would return in the spring to the new camp to resume their work.

Now that everybody was leaving, Pa decided it was time for him to file a claim with the government for the piece of land he had pointed out for their homestead on the southern edge of Silver Lake. To file the claim he had to travel to the land office in Brookings, forty miles away. While he was gone, he arranged for Robert Boast, a young Canadian-born man who had filed a homestead claim on some land on the east side of Silver Lake, to stay with Ma and the girls.

Laura liked Robert. He was tall and lanky and had the blackest eyes she had ever seen. He had a peculiar laugh that kept everyone entertained, and he liked to play games with Laura and her sisters.

When Pa arrived back from Brookings several days later, he had good news. Not only had he filed a claim for the land beside the lake, but also he had made a deal with the head surveyor of the railroad company. In return for the Ingalls family being allowed to move into the large, wood-frame surveyor's house for the winter, Pa would watch over the railroad company's property until after the spring thaw, when it could be transported west to the new camp.

Once again the Ingallses were on the move, but this time they had to travel only about fifty yards from their shanty to the surveyor's house. The new house was big and warm and snug, and Laura loved living in it. It had so much more room for everyone to spread out.

Soon after the Ingalls family had moved into the house, Robert Boast left the camp. He was headed to Iowa, where he planned to marry his fiancée, Ella, and bring her back to live at Silver Lake. Once he was gone, only Ma, Pa, Mary, Laura, Carrie, and Grace were left at the camp. For better or for worse, they were the six founding members of what would be a stop along the railroad track west—a stop that they hoped would soon be a town.

Chapter 11

The Long Winter

Just think!" Laura yelled as she whirled around and around on the grass outside the surveyor's house. "The nearest neighbor is twelve miles away, and it's forty miles to Brookings."

Mary laughed. "You always like to be in the middle of nowhere."

"And I always will," Laura said, tumbling to the ground. "I love to be outside. When I grow up, I'm never going to live in a town or a city. Who wants to hear the neighbors' baby crying or smell the smoke from someone else's chimney?"

"Or go to a library, or church, or listen to a concert," Mary added.

"Ma says all that will be here soon enough," Laura said gloomily.

Pa was sticking to his promise to Ma to settle down once and for all, and Laura knew that it was only a matter of a year or so before the place where she was standing would be swallowed up with buildings and people. Until then she intended to enjoy every minute of frontier life.

This was easy to do, living in such a grand house. The surveyor had originally intended to stay in the house through the winter, and so he had stocked it with canned food, flour, sugar, and sacks of potatoes. There was even a supply of coal to keep the family warm all winter. For the first time in Laura's life, Laura's mother was not concerned about how the family was going to make it through to spring.

Not only was there plenty of good food to eat during what turned out to be a mild winter, but also there were lots of things to do. Robert Boast returned just before Christmas with his new wife, Ella, and the couple moved into the shanty next door. Ella was just a few years older than Mary and lots of fun. She loaned the Ingalls family many books and newspapers, which Laura and her mother took turns reading aloud to Mary. Pa made a checkerboard, and sometimes Laura challenged Robert to a game. At other times Laura would sit by the attic window and look out across the vast expanse of white snow and wonder just what it would be like when a train finally chugged in from the east.

On February 7, 1880, Laura turned thirteen. Several weeks after her birthday, the first signs of spring began to appear. Wild geese started flying north, stopping off at Silver Lake, where they joined the swans and ducks that were also arriving. Laura struggled to find the words to describe to Mary the riotous scene of so many birds all floating on the lake. She was glad that at least her sister could hear the birds.

With the arrival of spring, people began to migrate west, and soon the surveyor's house became a hotel. Many of the people who stayed in the place were on their way to Brookings to stake a claim at the land office, or they were following the route of the railroad tracks west. Having people staying in the house kept Laura and Carrie busy helping Ma cook and clean throughout the day, and Pa kept the strangers from getting drunk and unruly at night. It frightened Laura to have so many people staying in the house, but she was glad for the money the visitors paid to be there: twenty-five cents for a meal, and the same again for a night's lodging.

If the strangers who stayed at the house had arrived one at a time, Laura might have been interested in them, but the sheer number of them coming overwhelmed her. One night a shoemaker from Wisconsin, a banker from Pennsylvania, and two printers from New York were all lodging at the house.

There was one guest who came to stay at the makeshift hotel whom Laura and her entire family were pleased to welcome. The man was the Reverend Mr. Alden, their old minister from Walnut Grove. Mr. Alden was just as surprised to see the Ingalls family as they were to see him. He was now a missionary in the Dakotas, traveling though the territory to see where to plant churches. He was sad to learn that Mary had become blind, though he informed Ma and Pa that a school for the blind was located in Iowa. Laura's heart raced as she heard this. She knew that Mary would love to continue her schooling if she could. Mr. Alden promised to find out how much it would cost to send Mary there.

Before he traveled on, Mr. Alden held the first church service in the small community. The service was held in the living room of the surveyor's house, and about twenty-five people crowded in together to sing hymns, hear a sermon, and listen to Mr. Alden talk about establishing a Congregational church nearby.

As the spring weather continued to warm, those arriving to make land claims and settle in the area were able to sleep outside in makeshift tents while they built their new homes.

One day in late March, Laura and Pa walked to the top of the low hill behind the old railway camp. At the top of the rise, Laura saw rows of sticks stuck into the ground.

"Those are surveyor's stakes, and this is where the town will be," Pa said, pointing to the sticks. "The courthouse will be over there to the west. And the main street runs along here."

Laura looked for a long time, but she could not imagine how these sticks were going to be transformed into a town. Still, as they walked among the surveyor's stakes, Pa's face began to light up. Finally Pa told Laura that it was too good of an idea to pass up. He had decided to take out another claim, this time on a piece of land right in the middle of the new community where he would erect a building that could serve as an office or a store. He explained that he would use wood and supplies from the old railroad shanties to build the place. When land in the new town got scarce, he planned to sell the building and make a handsome profit.

The next day Pa set out for Brookings to make his claim. When he returned, he announced that the new town was to be named De Smet, after a Belgian priest, Pierre De Smet. Father De Smet had worked among the local Dakota Indians in the 1840s and 1850s.

Laura helped her father whenever she could as he erected a structure on the land he had claimed in town. She watched as buildings sprang up like wildflowers on the prairie. Within three months of the surveyor's stakes being laid out on top of the hill, a town was born. Wood frame buildings were going up all along the streets the surveyor had marked out with his stakes. The main street of De Smet had been officially given the name Calumet Avenue, though Laura continued to refer to it as Main Street. And the street that ran past the new train depot that was being built was called First Street. Along Calumet Avenue a hotel was in the process of being built, along with a saloon, a hardware store, and a general store.

Each day Laura would look east and wonder when the railroad tracks would finally arrive in De Smet. Then one day she had to wonder no more. The crew laying the rails was on the outskirts of town. Laura walked down to the railway and watched the men work. The first thing the workers did as they were about to lay a new stretch of rails was to lay down sleepers at regular intervals. These were large slabs of hardwood that the rails would run on top of. When the sleepers were in place, several men carried a length of rail forward and placed it on top of the sleepers, being careful to align the end of it with the end of the rail behind it. Then they carried the second rail and laid it parallel to the other rail. While they did this, another group of men swooped into action. While two men, using metal plates and bolts, connected the new rail to the one behind it, several other men wielding heavy hammers drove metal spikes into the sleepers on either side of the rail. The spikes held the rail firmly in place so that the rail would not move sideways when a train ran along it.

In what seemed to Laura like no time at all, the railroad tracks through town were laid and the crew was on its way farther west. Following the crew down the tracks came a large, black locomotive that billowed smoke and belched steam. The locomotive pulled several flatcars and boxcars that were loaded with sleepers and lengths of iron rail and metal spikes and other tools and equipment the men needed to do their job.

With the rails in place, it was not long before trains were steaming into the train depot on First Street. The trains pulled boxcars filled with goods and carriage-loads of eager immigrants who spilled out onto First Street. Many of these new arrivals did not speak English, and they caused such a commotion when they arrived that Laura tried hard to avoid the train depot.

Then something terrible happened that compelled the Ingalls family to move out to the land they had claimed for their new homestead as fast as they could.

Pa arrived home ashen faced one day and told Ma, "There's been a murder."

Ma gasped, and a shiver ran down Laura's spine.

"Oh, Charles, who was it, and how did it happen? Ma finally asked.

"It was Jack Hunt."

Laura watched as Ma put her hand over her mouth in shock.

"Jack and his father had gone out to check on their land claim south of town. When they got there, they found that a claim jumper had taken over their shanty. As Jack opened the door to the shanty and stepped inside, the claim jumper shot him in the stomach. Jack's dad, who was still on the wagon, managed to whip the horses along and escape," Pa said.

"Did they get the claim jumper who shot him?" Laura asked.

"Yes. Jack's dad was able to report the shooting, and a posse went out and arrested the man," Pa said before going on. "You know, Caroline, I think we should move out to our land claim right away. What do you say?"

"Now?" Ma asked.

"The day after tomorrow," Pa replied. "With claim jumpers moving into the area, we need to be out on our land."

"The day after tomorrow, then," Ma said.

When Laura awoke the following morning, Pa was gone. Ma explained that he was at the land claim, building a shanty for the family to move into.

The following morning the Ingalls family loaded their belongings onto the wagon and headed out to their land claim. Although the shanty Pa had built the day before was not properly finished, the family moved into it anyway. The shanty had no door, and it still had gaps between the wallboards.

After the family had moved into the shanty, Pa set to work sealing the gaps and making the place waterproof by covering it with tar paper. Once he had finished the shanty, Pa turned his attention to the land. One of the conditions for being granted the land claim by the government was to clear and plow five acres of virgin prairie land during the first summer. Soon Pa was out working from sunup to sundown plowing the prairie. By the time he had finally turned the sod with the plow, it was too late to plant a wheat crop. Instead Pa planted turnips in the furrows.

Laura was amazed at how much work was involved in establishing the family on their new land. All Pa seemed to do was work, and in the evenings he was so tired that his fiddle never left its case for weeks on end.

Once the five acres of prairie had been plowed, it was time to build a barn and then to harvest hay from the long grass that grew along the edge of the lake. Laura felt sorry for her father as he labored away, and she offered to help him cut the long grass. Pa gladly accepted her offer, and the two of them worked from early in the morning until the sun began to set. Each night as Laura lay down to sleep, her muscles ached, but she told herself that the pain was worth the satisfaction of helping Pa.

As summer rolled by, Laura began to notice that there was less and less food on the table at each meal and that Pa was always the first to leave the table after eating only a few mouthfuls. At first Laura was puzzled by this, until she realized that Pa was leaving the table so that there would be more food for Ma and the girls to eat. Then one day Laura saw Pa snacking on some raw turnips from the garden, and she realized how hungry he must be. That was when she decided not to eat all her food, just like Pa, but leave some for the others to eat and to snack on raw turnips during the day when she was hungry. She had to admit, though, that raw turnips were not the tastiest of things to eat and took some getting used to.

Once the hay was harvested and stored away in the new barn, Pa began going into town regularly to do various carpentry jobs for people. This provided the family with a little more money for food and other necessities, which meant that Laura was able to give up eating raw turnips.

In October Pa decided that the family should move back into town for the winter. Some of the other families were intending to winter over on their land claims, but Pa feared that the coming winter might be a lot more extreme than the mild winter of the year before. He felt that if the winter was a lot harsher than the previous winter, the family would be safer in town than alone on the prairie in their shanty.

The Ingalls family packed up and moved back to De Smet. Though Pa's building in town was not quite finished, the family moved into it anyway. Even in its unfinished state, the building was more solidly built than the shanty. And the family could always get help from their town neighbors if they needed it.

Living back in town also meant the opportunity to attend the new De Smet school. Laura would just as soon have stayed home, but Ma insisted that she and Carrie attend class. After all, she told the girls, attending school was one of the main reasons that she wanted the family to stay in one place.

Fifteen children attended school, and as Laura surveyed them, she felt strangely out of place. She was the first girl in her class to have lived in De Smet, yet the town had grown so fast she hardly knew who lived in which house now.

School continued on until the end of November, when it recessed because of a passing storm. At least that is what it appeared to be at first. What started as a snowstorm soon turned into a howling blizzard. The blizzard raged for several days, piling up the snow in the streets of De Smet. Then as quickly as the blizzard had come, it left. Two days later, as people were still digging themselves out from all the snow that had fallen, another blizzard blew in from the north. For days the blizzard howled, and when it finally moved on, snow was piled up to the second story of the buildings in town. Laura had never seen so much snow piled like this in her life. Again, before the residents of De Smet could dig themselves out, another blizzard blew in, and then another one after that. In fact, it snowed so much that trains could no longer get through to the town. Laura heard one of the men in town tell Pa that snowdrifts forty feet high had blocked the railway.

December came and went, and still there was no letup in the constant flow of blizzards that hit the small town. Conditions were so desperate that Laura hardly noticed that Christmas had come and gone. With no trains getting through, supplies in town began to dwindle, and Laura had to get used to constant hunger pangs. To make matters worse, firewood was in short supply. The trees that had grown along the edge of Silver Lake by now had all been cut down, and the residents of the town were reduced to burning hay in their fireplaces. Laura was kept busy winding lengths of hay into sticks, or cats, as they were called, so that the hay would burn longer and hotter in the fireplace.

The pattern of blizzards continued on through January, with one blizzard followed by two days of respite and then another blizzard. In February things changed—but for the worse. February turned into one long blizzard. The wind howled, the snow piled up, and life was desperate and miserable for everyone in De Smet. Then in March the blizzards started to come less frequently, though it was still biting cold, and the Ingalls family stayed inside by the fireplace, trying to keep warm.

Finally, one day in April, Laura heard the most wonderful sound in the world—drip, drip, drip. It was the sound of snow and ice melting and dripping off the roof. Finally the spring thaw had come to De Smet, though things were still desperate in the town. Food supplies were virtually all used up. The last sack of wheat in the town had been sold back in December for fifty dollars. The trouble was, no one knew when the trains would be able to get through to De Smet with more supplies.

On May 10, 1881, nearly a month after the thaw had set in, the sound of a train whistle filled the air. Almost the entire population of De Smet headed for the train depot. They had hoped that the train was carrying boxcars full of grain and other foodstuffs, but they discovered that it was hauling machinery. However, the train was carrying some provisions for settlers farther west, and these were unloaded and divided among the people of town. It wasn't much, but it was enough to tide the people over until another train carrying food was able to make it to De Smet.

After the thaw, the Ingalls family moved back to their land claim. One day, at the end of May, Robert Boast and his wife, Ella, came to visit—it was time to finally enjoy Christmas dinner. Mr. Alden had sent along a plump turkey on the train, and Ma roasted it and served it along with all sorts of vegetables and corn cakes. As everyone sat around the table, Pa offered a blessing for the meal. "Lord, we thank Thee for all Thy bounty."

"Yes, and for bringing us safely through the long winter," Laura added under her breath.

Chapter 12

A Quiet, Steady Man

As wildflowers bloomed across the prairie, Pa kept busy plowing more land and planting a crop of wheat. When the wheat was planted he busied himself in town doing carpentry work. And there was plenty of work for him to do. It seemed to Laura that many people must have spent the long, hard winter planning for the future, because there were too many new building projects to count. Another bank, a post office, a dry-goods store, a meat market, a paint store, and a land office were all being built, and a number of existing stores installed board sidewalks outside so that customers did not have to trudge through mud during the thaw or when it rained. A grain silo was also erected so that the citizens of De Smet would not be caught without enough grain when the next barrage of blizzards roared down from the north.

Just as De Smet was changing, Laura sensed that her family also was changing. While her mother did not mention it often, Laura knew that Ma desperately wanted Mary to attend a seven-year course at the Iowa College for the Blind in Vinton, Iowa. Mr. Alden had returned with information on the school, as he had promised he would. He explained that the course offered practical training to a blind person, with lessons in how to read Braille, along with regular school classes in English, math, science, and geography.

Laura also wanted Mary to attend the school, and when Pa returned from town one night and announced that Mrs. White was looking for a seamstress assistant for the summer, Laura agreed to take the job. She did not enjoy sewing, as her mother did and Mary had, and she was sure that she would hate every minute of her new job. But at least the money she would earn would help her sister get the schooling she needed.

Laura was right; she did not like the job. Mrs. White put her straight to work making buttonholes in men's shirts. Since Laura was paid for each set of seven buttonholes she produced, she worked fast, neck bent, hands flying over the fabric. She hardly took the time to look up at the strangers who passed on the street, and when she went home each night, her fingers were raw and her back ached. Her only satisfaction each week was giving Ma her wages of a dollar and a half, which Ma carefully placed in a jar behind the fireplace.

At last, in November 1881, Pa and Laura had earned enough money to send Mary to Iowa. It was the loneliest moment of Laura's life as her parents helped Mary onto the train. As she watched the three of them through the window of the carriage, Laura knew that her family and her life would never be the same again. In seven years, when Mary would return to live with the family, Laura would be twenty-one years old! She could hardly imagine what might happen to her in that length of time.

As Laura walked back to the family's land claim with Carrie and Grace, she tried not to think about how different things would have been if Mary had not become blind, because when she did think about it, tears slid down her cheeks. Once back at the shanty, Laura had a lot to do. Ma and Pa had not hesitated to leave Laura—at fourteen years of age—alone in charge of her two younger sisters, the cow, the cooking, the cleaning, and the washing.

Laura was kept very busy, and she was glad when her parents arrived back a week later. They reported that Mary had settled into the school and was happy there. Now it was time for the Ingalls family to move back into town for the winter.

Thankfully, this winter proved to be a mild one, and Laura, Carrie, and Grace were able to attend school for much of it. At school they had a new teacher named Miss Eliza Jane Wilder. Laura did not like Miss Wilder one bit. Miss Wilder seemed to play favorites, and Laura was never on her favorite list. Even so, Laura did have a grudging admiration for the teacher's spunk. Ms. Wilder was older, in her thirties, and she had come west with her two younger brothers, Almanzo and Royal. All three of them had staked their own land claims, and Miss

Wilder had plowed her own fields and then planted, weeded, and harvested her own crops. Laura thought about the time that she had helped Pa bring in hay the year before, and she marveled at all her teacher had accomplished single-handedly.

Now that De Smet was bigger, there were many things to do during the long winter evenings. Sometimes Laura even had to choose between two events that were being held on the same night. There were sociables at the Reverend Brown's house, and Friday night literaries were held that featured singing, charades, and book readings. These events helped the family pass the winter in town until spring rolled around and they could move back out to their land.

Spring 1882 was much the same as the spring before, with two exceptions: Mary was no longer there, and Laura was studying hard. Laura did not want to study that hard, but she had decided she needed to. Very few jobs were open to a young woman on the frontier, and the one that paid the most money was schoolteaching. Even though Laura dreaded the idea of being cooped up in a classroom day after day, she had set her mind to passing the teaching proficiency test and was diligent in her studies over the next several months.

The Ingalls family once again moved back into town for winter. The new Congregational church building was now complete, and Laura's social calendar was fuller than ever. Her first activity was to attend a series of revival meetings at the new church at the end of October. Laura did not actually like the meetings, because everyone was supposed to pray out loud, which made her feel shy and awkward. But she went anyway because the gatherings were a way to meet all of the boys in town, and for the first time fifteen-year-old Laura Ingalls noticed them.

On the first night of the revival meetings, Laura was following her parents back down the aisle of the church when she felt a gentle tug on her sleeve. She turned to see Almanzo Wilder looking down at her.

"May I walk you home?" he asked.

Laura was too astonished to speak. She quickened her step and caught up to her parents. She felt her cheeks burn brightly as she walked home with them. By the time she reached the house, she had almost convinced herself that she had been hearing things. Almanzo, the younger brother of Miss Wilder, was ten years older than Laura. He was a man, a homesteader, and a daredevil horse rider!

The next night Almanzo asked again if he could walk Laura home, and this time she yes, she would be glad for an escort. Pa agreed as long as they did not dawdle on the way.

It was the same every night for the rest of the revival, and by the time the week was over, Laura had learned quite a lot about her teacher's brother. Almanzo had been born on February 13, 1857, in northern New York State. His parents had owned a large farm there, and he came from a family of three sisters and two brothers. His oldest sister, Laura Ann, was not much younger than Pa, and his youngest brother was a year younger than Carrie. Almanzo loved everything about farming, and all his life he had dreamed of becoming a farmer. When Almanzo was thirteen years old, his parents had moved west from New York to Spring Valley, Minnesota, where they had established another large farm. In 1879 Almanzo had come west to Dakota territory with his brother and sister, and they had made land claims on prairie land just north of what would become De Smet.

Soon after the revival meetings ended, the Ingalls family had an unfamiliar visitor. The man was named Louis Bouchie, and he came from a farm twelve miles south of De Smet. Laura did not like him from the first. His hair hung in stringy locks, and his clothes smelled as if they had not been washed since the previous Christmas. However, Laura sat patiently with Ma and Pa as Mr. Bouchie explained his mission.

"There are four of us with shanties out to the south. There were five families, but one of them abandoned their claim over the winter. So we all got together and thought we should turn the abandoned shanty into a schoolhouse. We have five school-aged children between us. Mrs. Bouchie and I have a small son, Johnny, but he is too young to attend school yet. My brother and his wife have three children, Ruby, Tommy, and Clarence, and the Harrisons have two children, Charles and Martha. All we need now is a schoolteacher, and I hear young Miss Ingalls is about ready to qualify as a teacher."

Laura looked down at her hands, unwilling to meet Mr. Bouchie's gaze. She waited for her mother to interject, to say that she was too young, that she was still in school herself, that she needed her to help with the younger children around the house, but her mother was silent.

Mr. Bouchie spoke again. "We can pay you twenty dollars a month for the two-month winter session. What do you say?"

Laura's mind raced. She was certainly not going to make forty dollars in two months doing anything else—not sewing buttonholes or making jelly to sell in town. She knew that Mary's tuition was due soon, and without giving it another thought, she set a smile on her face and announced, "Thank you, Mr. Bouchie. I would love to teach at your school. When do I start?"

"Give us one week, and we'll have the school-house spick-and-span and the children ready," Mr. Bouchie said. "Of course, you can board with my wife and me."

The next week was a busy one for Laura. She had been planning to become a teacher, but some-time in the future, not in a week! So much had to be done, the most important of which was for Laura to be certified as a teacher. The superintendent of schools for the county, Mr. Williams, came to the house to test Laura and issue her a teaching cer-tificate. He asked her many questions about English grammar, writing, arithmetic, geography, and his-tory. Laura easily passed the test. The only ques-tion Mr. Williams did not ask her was the one that mattered most—how old was she? The law stated that a person must be at least sixteen years of age to gain a teaching certificate, but Laura was still only fifteen years old. When Mr. Williams had finished giving the test, he signed the certificate that said that Laura was competent to teach school in the county.

At the end of the week, Pa took Laura out to the Bouchies' house in the sleigh. For mile after mile Laura stared out over the vast, snow-covered prairie, fretting about whether she would be able to control the students and teach them anything. After all, she was only a fifteen-year-old and not a very big one at that. Pa seemed to know what she was thinking, and as they approached the Bouchies' land claim, he leaned over and said, "You're a schoolteacher now, Laura. We knew that you would be one day, didn't we? We just didn't expect it to be so soon."

"Do you think I can do it, Pa?" Laura asked.

"Of course you can do it. You've never failed at anything you've tried to do in your life."

"But I've never tried schoolteaching," Laura said.

"No matter," Pa said. "I know you'll do a fine job."

Pa dropped Laura off at the Bouchies' shanty and then headed off home again so that he could make it back before dark.

The Bouchies' shanty was smaller than Ma and Pa's and not nearly as well built. A portion of the space had been divided off at the back, with a curtain to provide Laura living space. While the place seemed as cozy as a shanty could be in winter, Laura observed something cold about the way Louis Bouchie and his wife, Lib, related to each other. Mrs. Bouchie was sullen and brooding. She would often sit by the fire for hours and not say a word, and when she did speak, it was usually to yell and scream at Mr. Bouchie and their young son Johnny. In fact, the atmosphere inside the Bouchie household was so tense that it almost made Laura sick to her stomach. Laura was glad that Ma and Pa did not react to each other in such a way.

On Monday morning, the first day of school, Laura trudged through the half mile of snow to the schoolhouse. At first she had dreaded this moment, but with the situation as bad as it was at the Bouchies', she was glad to get away from the shanty. Suddenly teaching a class of students didn't seem that daunting.

Inside the schoolhouse a fire was roaring in the potbelly stove, and the students were already in class. But Mr. Bouchie had forgotten to tell Laura one thing about the students—three of them, two boys and a girl, were both taller and older than she was. Still, there was little Laura could do about it now. She pulled herself up to her full five-foot height and introduced herself as Miss Ingalls. Despite the fact that three of the children were older than she, the students were all polite and courteous as Laura taught them. In fact, Laura began to enjoy teaching the class, and the low part of her day came when she had to leave the schoolhouse and trudge back to the Bouchies' shanty.

Laura was delighted each Friday afternoon when Almanzo would pull up outside the schoolhouse in his cutter, a small sleigh pulled by one horse. Laura would climb in beside him, and he would ferry her home for the weekend. As she rode along, Laura poured out her heart to Almanzo. She told him everything—both the good and the bad—about living with the Bouchies and teaching school. Before long Laura was counting down the hours to each Friday afternoon when Almanzo would come to collect her in his cutter.

By the time the school term ended in late February, Laura was sixteen years old, though her experiences living in the Bouchies' shanty made her feel much older. And now that she was not teaching, she returned to attending school herself, as well as taking a job sewing buttonholes on Saturdays.

It was now three and a half years since Laura and her family had moved to De Smet, and Laura felt that her life was falling into a dreary pattern. Sometimes she attended school, sometimes she taught school in an outlying shanty for a few months at a time, and sometimes she did other work, like claim sitting for city folk who were too scared to spend the winter alone on the open prairie.

During 1883, Uncle Tom Quiner, Ma's brother, came through town with a wagon train of adventurers who were off to search for gold in the Black Hills of southwestern Dakota territory. Everyone was delighted to see Uncle Tom again. They were even more delighted when Mary also came home to visit. Laura was excited to find that her older sister had learned to read Braille and play the organ. Mary took her turn at church playing while the congregation sang, and Laura could see Pa's chest swell as he watched his oldest daughter's fingers darting over the keyboard. At that moment Laura knew that all of her sacrifices to send Mary to school had been worth it.

In October 1883, a letter arrived from Wisconsin to say that Grandma Laura Ingalls had died. Laura was sad when she heard the news. She hadn't spent much time during her life with her grandma, but what time she had spent with her had been delightful. The image of Grandma doing the jig at the sugaring-off dance was still burned in her memory.

The only consistent bright spot in Laura's life over the next year or so was the presence of Almanzo Wilder, or Manly, as she called him. Manly was always there to drive her to school or take her out to a land claim. He sat quietly beside her in church and listened attentively as she read poetry about the West. It did not happen overnight, but slowly Laura realized that she loved this quiet, steady man. When he asked her to marry him, she agreed.

The wedding was a simple affair. Eighteen-year-old Laura Ingalls and twenty-eight-year-old Almanzo Wilder stood before the Reverend Brown in his living room. One friend of Laura's and one friend of Manly's attended the service as witnesses. Mr. Brown read the vows, omitting the word *obey* at Laura's request, and then he declared Laura and Almanzo husband and wife.

When the simple service was over, Mr. and Mrs. Almanzo Wilder got in their buggy and rode out to Ma and Pa's farm for a celebration lunch. When the lunch was over, Laura and Manly climbed back into the buggy. There were tears and hugs as Laura said good-bye to her family and drove off. Manly headed

the horses over the familiar road that led to De
Smet. The newlyweds passed through town and
headed two miles north to their new home and a
new life together.

A week later their marriage was recorded in the
local newspaper.

> Married. WILDER-INGALLS—At the residence
> of the officiating clergyman, Rev. E. Brown,
> August 25, 1885. Mr. Almanzo J. Wilder and
> Miss Laura Ingalls, both of De Smet. Thus
> two more of our respected young people have
> united in the journey of life. May their voy-
> age be pleasant, their joys many, and their
> sorrows few.

Chapter 13

Joy and Sorrow

Manly was proud of the new house he took Laura to. He had built it with his own hands, and it sat in the middle of his tree claim. Laura loved the place from the start. The house was big and airy compared to Ma and Pa's shanty, and it had a neatly arranged pantry, complete with drawers and shelves set under a wide window. Laura would be able to look outside at the young trees growing while she kneaded bread dough or mixed cornmeal.

The tree claim was one of Manly's two land claims. His first claim consisted of 160 acres on which he had built a shanty, and he had already fulfilled the condition of breaking in a required portion of this land and been granted title to it by the government. The second land claim was known as a tree claim. To receive title to this 160 acres of land, Manly had to plant and grow ten acres of trees. The purpose in this requirement was to ensure that there would be adequate tree breaks on the open prairie. As a result, 3,405 trees were growing on ten acres of this land.

The day after her wedding, Laura Wilder began her new job as a farmer's wife. Manly was up before the sun, and Laura jumped out of bed after him, aware that it was her responsibility to light the stove and make him a hearty breakfast. Today the wheat was being threshed, so there would be a threshing crew to feed at dinnertime as well. Laura soon discovered that it was one thing to help Ma with the chores but quite another thing to be in charge of running a house yourself. She was embarrassed when the beans she served turned out to be as hard as pellets because she had not soaked them long enough, and the pie was tart because she had forgotten to add sugar to it. The threshing crew were good-natured about her mistakes. They laughed and promised to come back the next night to see if she had improved any.

For all of Manly and his threshing crew's hard work, the wheat crop was dry, and the price it fetched at market was low. However, this disappointment was offset by the good price Manly got for his field of oats, and plenty of hay was stacked in the barn for the winter.

The weather continued to be mild, and Manly had time to plow fifty more acres of his land. He worked from dawn to dusk doing it while Laura

worked just as hard cooking, churning butter,
sweeping, washing, ironing, and mending their
clothes. The monotony of the routine was broken by
Sunday-afternoon buggy rides. Manly had a knack
with horses, and Skip and Barnum, his two horses,
seemed to enjoy the outings as much as the young
couple did.

Soon, though, Manly decided he needed two
more horses. Skip and Barnum were not really big
enough to pull the plow, and if he was going to finish the plowing before the first snow fell, Manly
would need more horsepower. One day he went to
town and returned with two big horses and a new
McCormick plow.

Manly grinned from ear to ear as he explained
that the horses had been a real bargain and the
plow had cost fifty-five dollars but he had had to
pay only half that amount right now. The store manager was happy to extend him credit, and Manly
could pay the remaining money for the plow next
year, when a bigger crop of wheat would easily provide the money to pay for it.

Laura was a little surprised by this, and a twinge
of concern passed through her mind. However, she
decided not to entertain the concern. Manly was
twenty-eight years old, and he had done well up
until now without Laura's advice. Laura assured
herself that he did not need it now.

With the help of the new horses, Manly was able
to finish plowing before the first snow frosted the
ground. With the approach of colder weather, Laura
and Manly prepared to hunker down in their new

home for the winter. Laura set to work knitting socks for Manly and a fine undershirt for him that she hoped would be a Christmas surprise. It was not easy, however, to keep anything from him, since they were inside together much of the time. But as soon as Manly would go outside to check on the horses, Laura would pull out her knitting needles and complete a few more rows of the garment.

Christmas was a bright spot for the Wilders. The weather was mild, and Laura and Manly spent the day at the Ingallses' home. It felt like old times having the family sitting around the table, though Mary was back at college, and Manly sat in her place. Laura had ordered a set of dishes for her new house from the Montgomery Ward catalog, and the glassware had arrived by mail just in time to take to Ma and Pa's to show them.

The next celebration was Laura's nineteenth birthday, but since Manly would be turning twenty-nine a week later, the couple decided to celebrate both birthdays on the Sunday in between. For the occasion Laura made a dark chocolate cake, which they ate off their new glass dishes.

Several weeks after Manly and Laura's combined birthday celebration, the geese began flying overhead, headed north, and the prairie started to bloom. Spring had finally arrived, and Laura helped Manly plant wheat and oats in the fields he had plowed the previous fall. It was backbreaking work, and Laura ached all over. No sooner had she finished this task than she started to feel dizzy and found it hard to get out of bed in the morning. It took her a few days to work out what the problem was—she was pregnant!

Because of her pregnancy Laura could not work as hard as she had and was forced to take frequent rests. It was hard for her to look out the window and see Manly struggling alone with all the farm-work. The maple, elm, and cottonwood trees were not doing well in the hot weather, and Manly spent many hours mulching them with manure and hay from the barn.

In contrast, the wheat and oats were thriving in the hot weather and light summer rain. Manly declared that he had never seen such a good crop, and just as the wheat and oats were due to be har-vested, he went to town and bought a new har-vester. The machine cost two hundred dollars, but once again the store manager agreed to split the payments: one half when the crop was bought in, and the other half at the same time next year.

Laura was proud as she watched Manly hitch up the new harvester behind the horses. If he got through with harvesting the crops early enough, he planned to rent out the machine to their neighbors. In that way the machine could be paid for even sooner. Besides, Manly grinned, he had just heard that wheat was fetching seventy-five cents a bushel. Laura did some figuring in her head. They had one hundred acres planted in wheat. At forty bushels an acre, that added up to four thousand bushels of wheat. Four thousand times seventy-five cents was three thousand dollars! Laura worked the arith-metic backward to double-check herself, but she was right. In a month's time she and Manly would be able to pay off all their debts and still have plenty of money left over.

That day Manly cut fifty acres of oats and declared the new harvester to be the smoothest machine he had ever worked with. The next day he planned to cut the wheat, but when he found it still to be a little green, he decided to wait two days before harvesting it.

The day after he made this decision was stiflingly hot and unusually still. It looked like rain, but then the sky turned a pea-green color, and hail began to fall from the sky. At first the hail was the size of corn kernels, but as Laura and Manly watched in disbelief, the hailstones grew to the size of chicken eggs, pounding the crops mercilessly.

The hailstorm lasted only about twenty minutes, but when it was over, its damage was plain. Not a stalk of wheat was left standing; the wheat had all been pummeled to the ground by the hail. The hail had also stripped the young trees bare of all their leaves.

To add to the devastation of the event, Manly confessed that he still owed five hundred dollars on the house they were living in. He weakly told Laura that he had not wanted to bother her with such information. But now that money matters had become serious as a result of the loss of their crop of wheat, he would have to go to town the following morning and see what could be done about the situation.

Laura felt sick: the baby was due in December, they had to buy coal and provisions for the winter, and the three thousand dollars they were counting on had just evaporated.

When Manly left for town the next morning, Laura prayed that things would all work out somehow. And they did—sort of. The store manager agreed to extend the payments on the plow and the harvester, and Manly learned that he could sell any wild hay he harvested for four dollars a ton. He also found a couple willing to work the tree claim for a share of the profits from the land. This would free him and Laura to move onto his other land claim and farm it.

Within days Laura was packed up, and she and Manly moved to the other land claim, with its one-room shanty. It was August 25, and Laura and Manly remembered that it was their first wedding anniversary.

Together the couple harvested as much hay as they could, but it was not enough to meet the challenges of the coming winter. Manly arranged to mortgage the farm for eight hundred dollars, and with the money they were able to buy coal and pay the sixty dollars due in taxes.

Winter came, and on December 5, 1886, Laura realized that the baby was coming. Manly went to fetch the doctor and Ma, and they all returned in time for the child's birth. It was a girl, whom Laura named Rose, after her favorite flower. Laura was delighted to be a mother, though she gulped at having to pay the doctor one hundred dollars for his services. It seemed to her a lot of money for something as natural as childbirth. Still, Manly paid the bill, and Rose thrived through the harsh winter months.

The winter seemed to go on and on, and there was even a blizzard in April that killed two visitors to town. But finally the sun began to warm the ground again, and another cycle of farm life began. Nature was kinder this year, and Laura spent many happy hours outdoors, visiting with Manly and watching baby Rose. In the fall the price of wheat was lower, but there were no hailstorms, and the Wilders were able to harvest their crops and collect enough money to get them through the next winter.

The couple's second wedding anniversary came and went, as did Christmas and their joint birthday celebration. Then Laura became ill with a cold. Manly fetched Ma once again, and Ma took Rose back to the homestead so that Laura could rest.

Instead of getting better, however, Laura continued to feel worse, until she decided that the doctor would have to be called again, no matter how much it cost. The doctor's diagnosis was grave: Laura had diphtheria. Worse still, Manly was also coming down with the illness. Manly's brother Royal came to stay at the shanty and look after them both.

Laura was much sicker than Manly, though she did not know it as she drifted in and out of consciousness. She called for water and then refused to drink it when Royal brought it for her. But slowly she began to regain her strength and with each passing day became more conscious of what was going on around her. Finally Royal had to leave and go back to his land claim, so Manly crawled out of bed to tend to his and Laura's needs. The doctor had warned them both not to overexert themselves too soon, but it seemed they had little choice.

Ma brought Rose back to the shanty, and Laura loved hearing the patter of tiny feet around the house again. Then one morning Manly fell as he got out of bed. Laura watched as he tried to pull himself up, but he could not. He tried to move his legs, but they seemed to have no strength.

Alarmed, Laura rushed to him and pulled him onto the bed. She rubbed his legs, but Manly said he could not feel anything. Once again the doctor was called, only to learn the terrible truth. The doctor explained that Manly had most likely overexerted himself and suffered a stroke, but he could not rule out the possibility that Manly was suffering from polio. Either way, Manly would be partially paralyzed on the right side of his body for the rest of his life.

It was a crushing blow for Laura. Manly was only thirty-one years old, and now he could take on only the workload of an invalid. The couple who had been renting the tree claim had decided to head west, and there was no way that Manly could work both claims. And there was a new doctor's bill to pay. As soon as they were both well enough, Laura and Manly had to figure out what to do next.

The immediate answer came in the form of a homesteader from the East. The man offered to buy Manly and Laura's farm for one thousand dollars. Eight hundred dollars of the money would go to pay off the mortgage on the place, with two hundred dollars left over. They jumped at the opportunity, and once again Laura moved, this time back to the house on the tree-claim land.

It was like coming home again. Manly managed to get around a little more easily at the new house, since the land around it was more level than at the farm. Still, he struggled with lifting his feet high enough to get down steps or walk over a plank on the ground. A cane helped his mobility a little, but Laura found it hard not to cry sometimes when she watched him. Not only did Manly have trouble controlling his legs, but also he struggled to make small movements with his right hand. He could drive the horses, but Laura had to harness them for him, and he could eat with a spoon but could not cut up meat with a knife.

Despite his debilitating condition, Manly worked as hard as he could on the tree claim. Once again the summer was too hot for many of the trees, and he tried desperately to save them. Their crop of oats and wheat fared better.

That summer Laura and Manly also got involved in raising livestock. Laura's cousin Peter Ingalls had moved west and now lived a little north of them. Peter knew a man who wanted to sell one hundred head of purebred Shropshire sheep, and he proposed to Laura and Manly that they buy the sheep between them and raise them for wool. Peter had one hundred dollars to invest in the project, and by selling a horse that she had purchased with her wages from teaching before she was married, Laura raised the remaining money to invest in the scheme. A week later the sheep arrived, along with Peter, who had come to help raise them and do other chores with Manly.

Laura was delighted to have the extra company, especially when that extra help was her favorite cousin. Peter's arrival with the sheep seemed to bring good luck as the three adults struggled along together with the farmwork. The winter was mild, and by spring 1889 Laura was beginning to feel confident that they could make it after all. Lambing season had arrived, and there were so many sets of twins born that the flock of sheep doubled in size. The sheep were then sheared, and each fleece sold for about two dollars and fifty cents apiece. And something else good happened—Laura discovered that she was expecting another baby, and the child was due in midsummer.

Ma came to help out around the house whenever she could, and Carrie also came to visit and help. Then in August the baby arrived. This time Laura gave birth to a boy, and she was relieved when the child appeared to be healthy. She had been terrified that her diphtheria might have affected him.

Whether or not it had, no one could say for sure, but when the boy was twelve days old, he went into convulsions and died. Laura and Manly had not even agreed on a name for him yet. It was such a shock to Laura that she could hardly register what had happened. She sat woodenly as her dead baby was taken to the De Smet Cemetery and buried.

Following the burial Laura somehow managed to muster the strength to continue on cooking, cleaning, and looking after Rose, but all she did seemed mechanical to her. Then less than a week later, another tragedy struck. This time Laura was sweeping the bedroom when she smelled smoke. She opened the door and saw a wall of smoke—the house was on fire!

Quickly she scooped up Rose and ran out the door just as a neighbor ran up to help. Laura hardly noticed him. She flung herself down on the ground and screamed hysterically. She was screaming at the egg-sized hail, the diphtheria that had made Manly lame, the scorching sun that had withered the trees, the convulsing sickness that had killed her baby, and the flames that were now engulfing everything they owned. Her screams turned to sobs as she felt Manly's arm around her shoulder.

Laura watched in a blur as the house burned to the ground. Her neighbor had managed to reach in through the pantry window and rescue some silver cutlery and one of the dishes from her Montgomery Ward set of glassware. It was the oval bread plate, and around its rim were etched the words "Give us this day our daily bread."

Daily bread was about all the Wilder family had after that. They stayed with Ma and Pa for a while, and Manly and Laura's fourth wedding anniversary passed unnoticed. The family then went to stay with an old bachelor who needed a housekeeper. Laura and Manly exchanged their labor for food and shelter.

In his spare time, Manly laboriously managed to build another shanty on the tree claim, and the family was able to move into it in early winter. Throughout that winter Laura and Manly thought about what to do next. Manly was still a farmer at heart, but he was too discouraged to continue trying to make a living on this stretch of prairie. He wanted to go home to Minnesota, where he knew the land and the weather. Laura also was ready to leave, though she would rather have gone west than east.

As soon as it was warm enough in the spring, they sold the flock of sheep, their tree-claim land, and the farm equipment, and with the money they received they paid their debts. Laura said good-bye to her cousin Peter, who was heading off down the Mississippi River in search of adventure, and then she hitched up the wagon. As Laura packed up her few belongings, the newspaper clipping announcing her marriage fluttered out of her Bible and fell to the floor. She picked it up and read. "Thus two more of our respected young people have united in the journey of life. May their voyage be pleasant, their joys many, and their sorrows few." It seemed to Laura that the sorrows she and Manly had encountered so far had outnumbered the joys— about ten to one.

Chapter 14

A Real Home

The trip to Minnesota was a silent one. It reminded Laura of the one she had taken with her parents from South Troy, Minnesota, to Burr Oak, Iowa, after baby Freddie had died. But there were different ghosts along the way on this trip. Their route took them through Brookings and on into Minnesota, where they passed Plum Creek. The sod house on the creek bank had caved in by now, and as Laura looked at it, she marveled at how Ma could have made a hole in the ground into such a happy home. Things were certainly different for Laura now that her childhood was gone. The family stopped the night at Walnut Grove, though Laura stayed in the wagon on the outskirts of town. She did not want to talk to old friends. Then it was off across the prairie to eastern Minnesota and Manly's parents' farm in Spring Valley.

The farm was a pretty place, but Laura did not feel at home there, and Manly's leg and hand became more lame as winter set in. At a time when she was desperate to change their luck, Laura received a letter from her cousin Peter Ingalls. Peter explained how he had followed the Mississippi River all the way to the Gulf of Mexico and then traveled east, eventually settling in Westville, Florida. There he had met and married a backwoods girl named Molly, and now they had a baby on the way!

Laura looked up Westville on a map; the town was located in the middle of the panhandle of Florida, about 950 miles south of them. Peter ended his letter by inviting the Wilders to join him there. It was a startling invitation, but the more Laura and Manly discussed it, the more they liked the idea. The weather there was warm, and they could make a completely new start.

And so they did. In the summer of 1891, Laura, Manly, and Rose boarded a train for Florida. In the course of just two days they were transported from the prairie of the Midwest to the sandy pine- and palmetto-covered land of the Florida panhandle.

Peter met the Wilders at the train station and took them back to his small house. Laura immediately found the heat oppressive, and four-and-a-half-year-old Rose developed a prickly heat rash on her neck and body. Manly was the only one who liked the heat. As Laura suspected, it was good for his condition, and his legs and hand did not trouble him nearly as much.

Things about living in Florida other than the heat bothered Laura. Although the Civil War had ended twenty-six years before, the folks she tried to get to know made her feel as though it had ended only yesterday. They called Laura "Yankee girl" and made fun of her accent and manners. Some of their teasing was lighthearted fun, but some of it was not. As a result, Laura began carrying a loaded silver revolver in her pocket just in case she got into trouble.

Out West Laura had always turned to the outdoors for comfort—the beautiful sunsets streaking across the prairie, the ice melting in stony-bottomed creeks in spring—but in Westville the landscape was completely different and foreign to her. There were no clear, rushing streams, only lethargic, red-tinged rivers where alligators lurked, and huge cockroaches the length of a finger that scurried away when she walked through the scrub land. Other people might grow to love Florida, but Laura decided that she was not one of them. Neither was Manly. Although he felt better in the Florida heat, he could see no future in farming the land covered in pines and palmetto bushes that he was helping Peter to clear.

During their second summer in Florida, Laura grew ill from the humid heat and wanted to go home to De Smet. Manly agreed, and they gave the few possessions they had to Peter and Molly and boarded a train headed north. Laura, Manly, and Rose arrived back in De Smet in early August 1892, just in time for their seventh wedding anniversary.

Much had changed upon their return. The summer they had left turned out to be brutally hot, and many land claim stakers had decided to move on from the De Smet area. Even Pa had sold his homestead southwest of Silver Lake and had moved into

a new house he had built on Third Street. It was
the grandest house Ma and Pa had ever lived in. It
was a large, two-story wooden clapboard house with
a shingle roof. Downstairs were a parlor, two bedrooms, a kitchen, and a dining room. A twisting
stairway led upstairs, where there were three more
bedrooms. The backyard had a large garden and a
well with a hand pump. Laura was amazed at how
wonderful the house was. She decided it was Pa's
best carpentry work ever.

It was just as well that Pa had built a big house.
Mary had returned from the school for the blind in
Iowa and was now living back at home along with
Ma, Pa, Carrie, and Grace. Carrie was now twenty-
two years old and training to become a printer at
the local newspaper, while Grace was still attending
school.

For Laura it was wonderful to be home again
among her family. She and Manly rented a house
nearby to live in. Of course, there was also the matter of earning an income so that they could pay their
rent. Laura took a job with a local dressmaker,
sewing on buttons and basting seams, two things
she hated. Manly picked up odd jobs driving teams
of horses, serving as a clerk in a store, and doing
carpentry work like Pa did. Once the family had
settled into the house, Rose began attending school
and was looked after by Ma and Mary until Laura
came home in the evenings.

Every day as she went to work, Laura reminded
herself that their present circumstance was not a
permanent situation. She and Manly saved every

penny they could. They hoped to set out again soon in search of a place where they could both find happiness, a place that was not so hot and humid that it made Laura sick or so cold that it aggravated the pain in Manly's hand and legs.

It took two years, but eventually Manly and Laura had saved one hundred dollars, enough to launch out in their new plans. They loaded up their wagon and said good-bye to Laura's family. This time there was something final about the farewell, and Laura got goose bumps wondering whether she would ever see the members of her family again.

Rose clung to her Aunt Mary when it was time to go, and Laura hated to separate them. But soon the family were on their way once again, this time headed south through Nebraska and Kansas. They were not sure what they were looking for, but they had confidence that they would know it when they saw it.

In Kansas they turned east and crossed into southern Missouri. They passed through Spring-field and climbed into the rolling, tree-covered hills. They were in the Ozark Mountains, and as Laura and Manly looked at the beautiful country around them and breathed the clear, fresh air, they realized that this was country they could both enjoy. It was not too hot for Laura and not too cold for Manly. And when they reached the town of Mansfield, they realized they had found "home."

The Wilders camped on the outskirts of town, and the following morning they went in search of a farm to buy. They found what they were looking for

a mile east of town—forty acres of rocky hill country. Most of the land was covered in brush and
woods, but five acres of it had been cleared and
planted with apple trees. Among the apple trees
stood a windowless log cabin, much like the ones
Laura had lived in on the prairie as a child. Laura
immediately saw the potential of the land, and she
convinced Manly that they should buy it. Two days
later the Wilders moved onto their new farm, which
Laura affectionately named Rocky Ridge Farm.

At last Laura felt that she had found a real
home, though Manly needed constant reminding of
the land's potential during their first few months on
the farm. Laura told him that just because it was
not flat like the prairie they had grown up on did
not mean that it could not be productive. Perhaps
they might not be able to grow wheat and oats and
other crops as they had on the prairie, but the land
was good for raising cattle and sheep, and of course
there was the apple orchard. Manly nodded and set
about clearing more of the land.

After such a run of bad luck, it was almost
unbelievable to Manly and Laura that Rocky Ridge
Farm was paying for itself in just two years. The tiny
log cabin among the apple trees made a snug home.
Neighbors helped the Wilders construct a barn, and
Manly sowed grass seed for pasture on the land he
had cleared. He bought hogs and sheep and Jersey
cows to raise on the land. He also bought a fine
Morgan horse, a stallion that he used for breeding
in the hope of improving the quality of the horses
he saw throughout the area. Meanwhile Laura found

great delight in coaxing eggs from her leghorn hens and in helping Manly with the work outdoors. In the mild climate her garden bloomed, and soon her pantry was filled with canned plums, apples, grape jelly, and strawberry preserves.

When he had finished clearing the land, Manly started on building a proper frame house next to the log cabin. Together he and Laura felled the trees, cut the planks, and planed them until they were smooth. Then board by board over several years they built first one room, then two, then three. The first room they built became the new kitchen. An oak staircase was added that led to a second floor, with a bedroom for Rose. Laura found some big stones on the property and convinced Manly to hitch up the horses and drag them to the house, where they were set into the fireplace. Bit by bit the land and the house were turning into the home of Laura's dreams. The nightmares about fires and droughts, hailstorms, and grasshoppers faded, and Laura felt truly happy.

It was spring 1902 before something happened that upset Laura's world. Laura received word that Pa was sick and not expected to live long. She had not seen him since she had left De Smet eight years before, and she panicked at the thought of never seeing his face again. She threw some clothes into a bag and set out by train for De Smet. She made it there just in time to gather around the bed with her mother and sisters and see Pa smile as he recognized her. On June 8, 1902, soon after Laura had arrived, Charles Ingalls died.

It was a sad day for everyone, and particularly for Laura, as Pa's body was buried in the same plot as Laura's unnamed son. Grandfather and grandson were together in death. Following the funeral Laura returned to Rocky Ridge Farm with a broken heart. But slowly the work of tending the hens, raising motherless lambs, and currying the Morgan stallion soothed her spirits, and she was able to think back with gratefulness on all her wonderful memories of her father.

A visitor came to the farm that summer of 1902. It was Manly's sister Eliza Jane, who had been Laura's grouchy teacher all those years ago in De Smet. Eliza Jane had married, given birth to one son whom she had named Wilder, and become a widow since the last time Laura had seen her. Eliza Jane now lived in Crowley, Louisiana, and during her visit to Rocky Ridge Farm, she paid particular attention to fifteen-year-old Rose. Rose had always been an exceptionally smart girl, and Laura had seen to it that she attended the local school in Mansfield. But Eliza Jane insisted that a girl of Rose's potential needed a bigger, more challenging high school education. Reluctantly Laura agreed with her. As much as she had tried to interest Rose in farm life, her daughter was not interested in it one bit. Rose complained about the drudgery of cleaning out the chicken coop and the calluses she got on her hands from helping her father behind the plow. It was clear to everyone that Rose was not going to follow in the Ingalls or the Wilder tradition of pioneer farming. With a heavy heart, Laura and

Manly let their daughter go to Crowley with her Aunt Eliza Jane.

With Rose gone, Laura and Manly had as much work as ever to do, and they filled up their days working happily together. Rose wrote to them regularly, announcing one week that she had won an essay competition and then in her next letter that she had received a ribbon for being first in her class in English and Latin. She wrote of wanting to become a writer, clearly something that she was suited to. When she finished high school, she took a job as a telegrapher at Western Union. She was seventeen years old, and Laura was sure that her daughter was destined for a more adventurous life than Crowley could offer her.

In 1906 Rose moved to San Francisco, California, and became one of the first female real estate agents there. She grew rich and popular. Neither Laura nor Manly was surprised when in March 1909 she wrote to say that she was marrying a local San Francisco man named Claire Lane. The new couple's relationship was rocky from the start, and it grew more tense when Rose's son died soon after his birth the following year. Laura was heartbroken for her daughter. She recalled the pain of losing a brother and a son herself. She wrote to Rose, urging her to pursue her interest in writing.

Meanwhile Laura's reputation as a fine farmer's wife was spreading, and Laura was being invited to speak at farmers' meetings and conventions. Her specialty topic was raising hens for maximum egg production. Laura had also involved herself in many other activities that benefited the lives of country women, such things as organizing clubs, helping to set up public libraries, and establishing a branch of the Red Cross.

By 1911 Laura was in such demand as a speaker that she could not attend every function she was invited to speak at. When she could not show up in person, she often would write down her thoughts on the specified topic and send them along to be read in her absence. She did not think much of doing this until a man named John Case wrote to her. Case was the editor of the *Ruralist*, a newspaper produced for farmers in Missouri, and he had heard one of Laura's papers read aloud at a conference he had attended. Laura was stunned as she read on and learned that Case wanted her to write a weekly column for his newspaper. Laura said yes to the offer. She was forty-four years old, and although she did not know it then, she had just set course on the most exciting adventure of her life.

Chapter 15

Old Things Passing Away

Laura continued to write her column for the *Ruralist* and keep up with the many tasks of a farmer's wife. In her spare time she kept in touch with her family by letters. She found Carrie's letters especially interesting. Carrie had moved around, working for various independent, liberal newspapers, and had eventually settled in Keystone, located in the Black Hills of South Dakota. It seemed to Laura that writing genes—or at least storytelling genes—flowed in the Ingalls blood. In 1912 Carrie wrote to say that she had married a widower from Keystone named David Swanzey, who had two young sons. Ma and Mary continued to live together in the house on Third Street in De Smet, and Grace had married a local De Smet farmer named Nathan Dow.

In 1915, Rose invited her mother to visit her in San Francisco, where she was now a writer for a newspaper. Laura was anxious to see how her daughter was getting on. Manly stayed behind to take care of the farm, and Laura promised as she climbed aboard the train for the journey west to write him lots of letters. Rose met her mother at the station, and the two of them spent the next week together exploring San Francisco. They visited the Panama-Pacific Exposition being held in the city. They went to Chinatown and Golden Gate Park. Laura stood on the western edge of the American continent and felt the cold water of the Pacific Ocean wash over her feet. Laura often thought of Pa and how he would have loved to have made it all the way west to the Pacific Ocean. What adventures he could have had there!

Rose also showed her mother the newspaper office where she worked and let her read some of the articles she had written for the newspaper. Laura was very proud that her daughter had a talent for writing.

In 1920, after Rose had divorced her husband, she headed overseas. The Great War was over in Europe, and Rose wanted to be a part of document-ing what had happened and helping in the rebuild-ing. She found a job as a publicist for the American Red Cross in Paris and used that city as a base from which she traveled to much of the world. Laura and Manly grew used to receiving postcards from Rose from such faraway places as Hong Kong, Albania, and Egypt. It seemed to Laura that Pa's moving-around bug was very much alive in his grand-daughter.

Christmas 1923 was an exciting time for Laura. Rose was coming home! She was thirty-seven years old now, and thanks to the feature articles she had written about her travels, she was also a famous American writer. Laura and Manly met their daughter at the train station in Mansfield. Laura ordered a taxi to take her and Rose from the station to the farmhouse while Manly followed along more slowly in the lumbering old wagon filled with Rose's trunks. Over a dinner of chicken pie and apple dumplings, Rose said to her parents that she would like to stay at Rocky Ridge Farm for a year. She explained that she had two purposes in mind in doing this. First, she wanted to spend time with her parents, and second, she wanted to write and sell enough magazine articles about her travels to provide Laura and Manly a comfortable financial cushion and retirement fund. Manly helped set up her typewriter in her old bedroom, and Rose was soon busy typing away.

One of the stories Rose wrote while at the farm was purchased by *Country Gentlemen* magazine, to be produced in serial form. Rose received a check in the mail for ten thousand dollars for her story. Laura was staggered by the amount. It was nothing like the sort of money she was being paid by the Missouri *Ruralist* for her articles! Rose encouraged Laura to branch out and try writing for bigger newspapers, but Laura was reluctant to leave the world of chickens and fences and lemon curd pie recipes.

Rose was full of other ways to improve her parents' lives. One of these improvements was the gift of a 1923 blue Buick motorcar. Laura was astounded when Rose drove the vehicle up their drive and parked it in front of the house. She knew that Rose drove a car, but she had never actually seen her behind the wheel of one before.

Manly was eager to try his hand at driving, but he learned the hard way how different it was from driving a team of horses. Rose took him for a lesson, and when he got into a sticky situation, he tried to do the same thing he would have done on a wagon to bring it to a halt, slamming his foot hard on the wagon brake and pulling back on the reins. In the car, however, this reflex had Manly slamming his foot down hard on the accelerator and pulling up on the steering wheel with all his might. The Buick lurched forward and crashed into a tree, but the car was soon repaired, and the lessons continued. Laura decided that she would be just as good a driver as Manly. After all, he was sixty-six years old, and she was only fifty-six. Rose also gave her mother lessons, and soon both Laura and Manly were confidently driving into Mansfield and back.

Along with the joy of having Rose home again came a fresh heartbreak for Laura, who received a telegram telling her that Ma had died on Easter Sunday 1924. Since Laura did not have enough time to make arrangements to get back to De Smet for the funeral, she mourned privately. She thought of how her ma had always tried to be happy and positive, how she had encouraged her children and wanted the best for them. She thought about how difficult Ma's life had been and how Ma had bravely borne her troubles so that her children were often sheltered from adult worries. She also thought about Ma and Pa's children. Freddie had died as a baby, but Ma and Pa had had four daughters. Of those daughters, Laura was the only one who had a child of her own, and Rose had no living children. It seemed hard for Laura to believe that Pa's line of Ingallses would die out with Rose.

Mary wrote soon after the funeral to say that the house on Third Street in De Smet had been sold and she had moved to the Black Hills to be with Carrie and her husband.

After a year at home, in late 1924, Rose moved on to New York City, where she met with a literary agent. She wrote back to say that the agent had commissioned Laura to write two articles, one on her newly remodeled farm kitchen and the other on the farmhouse dining room. Rose provided detailed instructions on what Laura needed to cover in the articles and how to take the photographs that would be needed to accompany them. Rose concluded her letter with the words, "What I am trying to do is give you the benefit of these ten years of work and study. I'm trying to train you as a writer for the big market. Here is your chance...to make a real income.... Get yourself free to go after this. There is no reason under heaven why you should not be making four or five thousand dollars a year."

Laura smiled to herself as she read the words. She had become the student, and her daughter, the teacher. She followed Rose's instructions carefully, and in January 1925 the article "My Ozark Kitchen" was published. Being published was a big step for Laura, who chose to use a new byline for the article. In her *Ruralist* writings she had always gone by the name Mrs. A. J. Wilder. Now, in honor of her family roots, she attributed the article as being by Laura Ingalls Wilder.

The second article, "The Farm Dining Room," followed in June. *Country Gentlemen* magazine paid Laura $150 for each article. This was the easiest money Laura had ever earned.

The timing of the article writing was perfect. Laura knew that she and Manly needed to slow down their busy farm schedule, and the two articles plus others that Laura wrote soon afterward helped supplement their income.

With Rose having moved east and with Ma dead, Laura found herself thinking more and more about the past. It was not even thinking about it, really. At odd moments of the day, it was as if she were back there again. She would be running down the side of the dugout at Plum Creek, pulling back the weeping willow branches to make a stage with Mary, helping Pa bring in the hay at the homestead by Silver Lake, or sitting in Miss Eliza Jane's school-room, reciting spelling lessons. At times the past seemed more real to Laura than the present. This was especially true when she heard that Mary had died of pneumonia on October 17, 1928. Laura felt an acute sense of the old things passing away— away into oblivion unless someone captured them before it was too late.

Eventually, at over sixty years of age, Laura decided that she was up to the task. She would retell the family stories as a way of preserving the life and people she had known and loved. One morning, after the dishes were done and the potatoes peeled for lunch, Laura slipped into her corner study and sat down at the desk Manly had made for her. She pulled out a thick, yellow writing tablet, sharpened a pencil, and began to write. "Once upon a time, sixty years ago, a little girl lived in the Big Woods of Wisconsin, in a little gray house made of logs." Laura wrote for an hour without stopping. She discovered that having been Mary's eyes for so many years had made it easy for her to describe things on paper. It was as if the stories were waiting for her to write them. She told about the long winter days and nights, about Christmastime, and about her grandpa collecting sap from the maple trees and making maple syrup and sugar.

When she put down her pen, Laura was satisfied with the start she had made. She liked the way she wrote about the little girl named Laura as if it were someone she was observing and not herself. She knew that much of that Laura was her, but parts of that Laura were not. It was so freeing not to be writing a history or a biography but simply telling stories about her life. Since they were stories, she could change the names of people if she thought it best or change people's ages, or even some of the things that happened to them. And she could leave out the saddest stories, like the one about Baby Freddie's dying. That was not something she ever wanted to retell for her audience.

But whatever Laura changed, she knew one thing: she would write only about things that had happened either to her or to someone she knew.

When she was finished telling all that she wanted to tell, Laura sent the manuscript to Rose, who helped her revise it. Rose then passed the manuscript on to an editor at Harper and Brothers publishing house in New York City. The editor, Virginia Kirkus, loved the stories and wrote to Laura to offer her a contract. Virginia explained that a book like Laura's was just what the public needed these days. A serious depression had just hit the United States, and people needed reminding that it was the simple things in life that were the most important.

Laura heartily agreed and signed the contract. Within a year the book, titled *Little House in the Big Woods*, had been published and was on bookstore shelves. It was an instant sensation, and children began writing to Laura, begging her for more stories.

This turn of events caught Laura by surprise. Laura had not imagined writing more than one book. Now sixty-five years old, she had not intended starting a new career! But she started to think of other stories that she had not yet told, stories about her time at Plum Creek and Silver Lake and the long, harsh winter they had endured. She also thought about Manly's life and how interesting that would be to children, and she decided to make that her next book.

Laura watched as Manly's eyes often misted over as she questioned him about the things he remembered. From his memories she wrote a book that she entitled *Farmer Boy*. The book was published in 1933. But *Farmer Boy* did not stop the flow of letters Laura received asking questions about her life and the life of her family. So Laura kept on writing. Her next book, published two years later, was titled *Little House on the Prairie*. This book was followed by *On the Banks of Plum Creek* in 1937.

By now Laura was in high demand as an author, and her publisher sent her on a book tour to Detroit. While in Detroit Manly and Laura visited the Henry Ford Museum. They loved walking around the place, viewing the exhibits. Manly was particularly intrigued by the display of what were considered "antique" farm implements. "I remember using a great many of these implements," he told Laura. "Maybe I should be a museum exhibit."

In Detroit Laura gave a speech at the Children's Book Fair on why she wrote her books. "We had a busy, happy childhood," she said, "but of it all, sister Mary and I loved Pa's stories best. We never forgot them, and I have always felt that they were too good to be altogether lost. Children today could not have a childhood like mine in the Big Woods of Wisconsin, but they could learn from it and hear the stories that Pa used to tell."

Laura went on to explain that as she reflected back over time, she realized she had a unique point of view.

I began to think what a wonderful childhood I had had. How I had seen the whole frontier, the woods, the Indian country of the great plains, the frontier towns, the building of railroads in wild, unsettled country, homesteading and farmers coming in to take possession. I realized that I had seen and lived it all—all the successive phases of the frontier, first the frontiersman, then the pioneer, then the farmers, and the towns. Then I understood that in my own life I represented a whole period of American history.... I wanted the children now to understand more about the beginnings of things, to know what is behind the things they see—what it is that made America as they know it.

When they got home to Rocky Ridge Farm from the book tour, Laura put the finishing touches to the manuscript for *By the Shores of Silver Lake* and submitted it to her publisher.

By way of celebration for the publication of the book, Manly suggested that he and Laura visit De Smet for Old Settlers Day. Laura was enthusiastic. An adventure was just what she needed, and writing about the town had made her homesick to see the old sights. Grace and her husband also lived in De Smet, and Laura looked forward to visiting with her sister.

Laura and Manly set out early one morning from Rocky Ridge Farm, with eighty-two-year-old Manly driving their Chrysler motorcar. Manly managed to get lost three times that first morning, and Laura wondered whether they would ever make it to De Smet. Manly's navigating skills improved, and the couple arrived there in time for the event. They took a room in a hotel in De Smet just down the street from where Pa's office building had once stood. A large brick bank building with offices above now stood on the site. Laura and Manly could hardly believe how big De Smet had become. The town stretched far beyond the railway to the north and spread all the way east to the edge of the lake. Laura and Manly visited Pa and Ma's homestead, which brought back a flood of memories for Laura. A large wood-frame farmhouse now stood on the site of the old shanty the Ingalls family had lived in.

On the street Laura often heard her name being called. She would turn around to look into an old, graying face and struggle to connect the face with that of a child or teenager who lived in her memory. It disturbed her to think that she looked just as old as these other people looked when she still felt so young at heart. But once Laura had adjusted to how old everyone had grown, she enjoyed many happy reunions with old friends.

After visiting with Laura's sister Grace and her husband, Laura and Manly drove west across South Dakota to the Black Hills to visit Carrie and her husband. After visiting with Carrie, they drove on to Wyoming and then down the Rocky Mountains to Colorado Springs. From there they headed east across Colorado and Kansas before making it back safely to Rocky Ridge Farm.

The journey had been a wonderful adventure, but upon their return, Laura sensed that their traveling days were over. She and Manly had visited the

"Land of Used-to-Be," as Laura called it, and had found that many things had changed. Laura found it much more rewarding to revisit the places that existed in her memory and to write about them for her readers. With renewed vigor she set to work and wrote *The Long Winter* in 1940 and *Little Town on the Prairie* in 1941. Two years later, with the publication of the *These Happy Golden Years*, a book about her teenage years, Laura's writing days were over.

The same year that Laura wrote *Little Town on the Prairie*, her sister Grace died, followed in 1946 by Carrie. At seventy-nine years old, Laura was now the only member of her family left. It gave her great satisfaction to think that, through her books, some part of her family's lives would go on for a long time to come.

Three years later, Manly suffered two heart attacks. He fought valiantly to regain his strength after them, but it was not to be. Almanzo Wilder died on October 23, 1949, at the age of ninety-two. He was buried in the local cemetery in Mansfield, Missouri.

Laura had lost her partner of sixty-four years. Sometimes she wondered if it could really have been that long ago that she and Manly had moved into the house on the tree claim. How dashing he had been when he came for her in his wagon pulled by perfectly groomed Morgan horses, and how patient and uncomplaining he had been through all his suffering.

As Laura thought about Manly, she drew inspiration to go on. She still had things to live for. Rose was busier than ever with her writing, and hundreds of letters poured into the Mansfield post office each week for Laura. The fan letters bore postmarks of places from Alaska to Texas to New York City.

On February 7, 1957, Laura celebrated her ninetieth birthday. She thought back on the birthdays she had enjoyed as a child. How long ago and far away her childhood now seemed. Three days later Laura fell asleep in her bed at Rocky Ridge Farm. She did not wake up the following morning. Sometime during the night she had died peacefully in her sleep. Laura was buried beside Manly in the local cemetery in Mansfield.

Two books were published after Laura's death: *West From Home: Letters of Laura Ingalls Wilder to Almanzo Wilder, San Francisco, 1915* and *The First Four Years*, a book about the difficult early years of her marriage. Laura had written this manuscript by hand in several notebooks but had never shown it to anyone. Rose found the manuscript among her mother's belongings.

So much of Laura Ingalls Wilder still remains today: in her books, in the television series that was based on her stories, and in the imaginations of countless children to whom she brought history— her history—to life.

Anderson, William. *Laura Ingalls Wilder Country*. New York: HarperPerennial, 1990.

Hines, Stephen W. *I Remember Laura: Laura Ingalls Wilder*. Nashville: Thomas Nelson Publishers, 1994.

Wilder, Laura Ingalls. *By the Shores of Silver Lake*. New York: Harper & Brothers, 1939.

Wilder, Laura Ingalls. *Farmer Boy*. New York: Harper & Brothers, 1933.

Wilder, Laura Ingalls. *The First Four Years*. New York: Harper & Row, 1971.

Wilder, Laura Ingalls. *Little House in the Big Woods*. New York: Harper & Brothers, 1932.

Wilder, Laura Ingalls. Edited by Stephen W. Hines. *Little House in the Ozarks: The Rediscovered Writings*. Nashville: Thomas Nelson Publishers, 1991.

Wilder, Laura Ingalls. *Little House on the Prairie*. New York: Harper & Brothers, 1935.

Wilder, Laura Ingalls. *Little Town on the Prairie*. New York: Harper & Brothers, 1941.

Wilder, Laura Ingalls. *The Long Winter*. New York: Harper & Brothers, 1940.

Wilder, Laura Ingalls. *On the Banks of Plum Creek.* New York: Harper & Brothers, 1937.

Wilder, Laura Ingalls. *These Happy Golden Years.* New York: Harper & Brothers, 1943.

Wilder, Laura Ingalls. *West From Home: Letters of Laura Ingalls Wilder to Almanzo Wilder, San Francisco, 1915.* New York: Harper & Row, 1974.

Wilder, Laura Ingalls and Rose Wilder Lane. Edited by William T. Anderson. *A Little House Sampler.* Lincoln: University of Nebraska Press, 1988.

Zochert, Donald. *Laura: The Life of Laura Ingalls Wilder.* Chicago: Henry Regnery, 1976.

Janet and Geoff Benge are a husband and wife writing team with twenty years of writing experience. Janet is a former elementary school teacher. Geoff holds a degree in history. Together they have a passion to make history come alive for a new generation of readers.

Originally from New Zealand, the Benges make their home in the Orlando, Florida, area.

Also from Janet and Geoff Benge...

More adventure-filled biographies for ages 10 to 100!

Abraham Lincoln: A New Birth of Freedom • 1-883002-79-6
Adoniram Judson: Bound for Burma • 1-57658-161-6
Amy Carmichael: Rescuer of Precious Gems • 1-57658-018-0
Benjamin Franklin: Live Wire • 1-932096-14-0
Betty Greene: Wings to Serve • 1-57658-152-7
Brother Andrew: God's Secret Agent • 1-57658-355-4
Cameron Townsend: Good News in Every Language • 1-57658-164-0
Clara Barton: Courage under Fire • 1-883002-50-8
Corrie ten Boom: Keeper of the Angels' Den • 1-57658-136-5
Christopher Columbus: Across the Ocean Sea • 1-932096-23-X
Clarence Jones: Mr. Radio • 1-57658-343-0
Count Zinzendorf: Firstfruit • 1-57658-262-0
C.T. Studd: No Retreat • 1-57658-288-4
Daniel Boone: Frontiersman • 1-932096-09-4
David Livingstone: Africa's Trailblazer • 1-57658-153-5
Douglas MacArthur: What Greater Honor • 1-932096-15-9
Eric Liddell: Something Greater Than Gold • 1-57658-137-3
Florence Young: Mission Accomplished • 1-57658-313-9
George Müller: The Guardian of Bristol's Orphans • 1-57658-145-4
George Washington: True Patriot • 1-883002-81-8
George Washington Carver: From Slave to Scientist • 1-883002-78-8
Gladys Aylward: The Adventure of a Lifetime • 1-57658-019-9
Harriet Tubman: Freedombound • 1-883002-90-7
Hudson Taylor: Deep in the Heart of China • 1-57658-016-4
Ida Scudder: Healing Bodies, Touching Hearts • 1-57658-285-X
Jim Elliot: One Great Purpose • 1-57658-146-2
John Adams: Independence Forever • 1-883002-51-6
John Williams: Messenger of Peace • 1-57658-256-6
Jonathan Goforth: An Open Door in China • 1-57658-174-8
Hudson Taylor: Deep in the Heart of China • 1-57658-016-4
Laura Ingalls Wilder: A Storybook Life • 1-932096-32-9
Lillian Trasher: The Greatest Wonder in Egypt • 1-57658-305-8
Lottie Moon: Giving Her All for China • 1-57658-188-8

Mary Slessor: Forward into Calabar • 1-57658-148-9
Meriwether Lewis: Off the Edge of the Map • 1-883002-80-X
Nate Saint: On a Wing and a Prayer • 1-57658-017-2
Rachel Saint: A Star in the Jungle • 1-57658-337-6
Rowland Bingham: Into Africa's Interior • 1-57658-282-5
Sundar Singh: Footprints Over the Mountains • 1-57658-318-X
Theodore Roosevelt: An American Original • 1-932096-10-8
Wilfred Grenfell: Fisher of Men • 1-57658-292-2
William Booth: Soup, Soap, and Salvation • 1-57658-258-2
William Carey: Obliged to Go • 1-57658-147-0
William Penn: Liberty and Justice for All • 1-883002-82-6

Also available:

Unit Study Curriculum Guides

Turn a great reading experience into an even greater
learning opportunity with a Unit Study Curriculum Guide.
Available for select biographies.

Available from YWAM Publishing
1-800-922-2143 / www.ywampublishing.com